WILLIAM BLAKE

William Blake

by MARTIN K. NURMI

THE KENT STATE UNIVERSITY PRESS

First published by Hutchinson & Co.
(Publishers) Ltd. 1975
U.S. edition by The Kent State
University Press 1976

Library of Congress Cataloging in Publication Data

Nurmi, Martin K
  William Blake.

  Bibliography: p.
  Includes index.
  1. Blake, William, 1757–1827.
PR4146.N8   1976   821'.7   76-25476
ISBN 0-87338-191-2
ISBN 0-87338-192-0 pbk.

For Ruth

Contents

	Preface	9
	Author's note	10
1	Some biographical facts	11
2	*Poetical Sketches* and other early works	35
3	Early works in 'Illuminated Printing'	50
4	*The Marriage of Heaven and Hell*	70
5	Political prophecies	85
6	The shorter prophecies	105
7	*The Four Zoas*	119
8	The last prophecies	146
	Notes	162
	Suggestions for further reading	167
	Index	170

Plates

facing page

1. Portrait of William Blake by John Linnell (by courtesy of the Fitzwilliam Museum, Cambridge).   64

2. 'The Sick Rose' from *Songs of Experience* (by courtesy of the Trustees of the British Museum).   65

3. Plate from *The Book of Urizen* (by courtesy of the Trustees of the British Museum).   96

4. Title-page from the uncoloured version of *Jerusalem* (by courtesy of the Trustees of the British Museum).   97

Preface

'I give you the end of a golden string,' said Blake,

> Only wind it into a ball:
> It will lead you in at Heavens gate,
> Built in Jerusalems wall.

Unfortunately, some readers coming to Blake for the first time have had the impression that the string may have more than the usual number of ends and have felt the need for some help in being introduced to him. This is what I have tried to provide both for the student and general reader in this introduction. Some of what I have said has been said before more fully in specialized and advanced studies which take more knowledge for granted. What I hope to have provided is an introduction to Blake's poetry—it has not been possible to give much attention to his art—and also an introduction to essential but demanding works like Northrop Frye's *Fearful Symmetry* and David V. Erdman's *Blake: Prophet against Empire*, to both of which any student of Blake must be heavily indebted. In trying to make Blake's poetry more easily accessible, I hope I have not diminished the wonder of his difference from most other poets but only clarified it a little.

To Professor Erdman I owe a deep debt of gratitude extending from the time when he first introduced me to Blake. I am also indebted to the Research Committee of Kent State University for a grant of time and to Professors Donald Ault and William Hildebrand for useful suggestions. I am greatly indebted to Professor John Lawlor, who read the manuscript with great care and made a host of valuable suggestions. But first and last there is Ruth, who is Oothoon and Enitharmon.

9

Author's Note

Quotations from Blake's work are from David Erdman's edition. Page references will be given to this and to Geoffrey Keynes' edition, and abbreviated as E 600; K 133.

I | Some biographical facts

Not many years ago, William Blake was known generally as a strange 'mystical' English poet of the late eighteenth and early nineteenth century, who wrote some simple but mysterious lyrics called *Songs of Innocence and of Experience*, notably 'The Tyger', and then somehow lost his true calling as a lyricist in the impenetrable forests of his so-called 'prophetic books', which very likely were the products of a severe if amiable mental illness. He made many critics uneasy because he seemed so different from other poets of his time, and a fairly typical reaction to this uneasiness was that adopted by Mr E. M. Forster, who in a review advised his reader 'to read him, don't talk about him'. Forster handled the later works by saying that Blake 'gets a bore' in them.[1] Blake seemed not to belong either to the eighteenth century, in which he was born and produced a good deal of the work by which he is chiefly re-membered, or to the Romantic period, in which he wrote the works he considered his major ones. He was anthologized in collections for both periods, but it was evidently possible even fifteen or twenty years ago to consider the major poets of the Romantic period and leave Blake out, as was done, almost officially, in the Modern Language Association of America's first guide to research in the Romantics, *The English Romantic Poets: A Review of Research*, 1950. It was even possible in courses of study for advanced degrees to specialize in the Romantic period without being responsible for any real knowledge of Blake.

This is no longer true, among either the scholarly community or the intelligent reading public. Blake was hard to get to know, but through the energetic efforts of at first a relatively small band of scholarly critics he was made accessible for study even in cram

1. Superior figures refer to Notes, pp. 162–166.

courses in our universities. He is demanding but no longer so odd, or frightening, that anyone should be enjoined simply to read him but not feel obliged to talk about him—though 'The Tyger' is still occasionally said to defy critical analysis, as perhaps it does. Blake has been fortunate in some of his critics, who have built up a solid body of sound critical and scholarly information that is capable of transmission and of being added to. As a result of all this, he has emerged as indeed a major poet, very much of his time, embodying in rich if sometimes extreme form—rich, perhaps, *because* extreme— the characteristics of the Romantic movement, showing clear parallels with at least Shelley and Byron. In fact, a few critics have gone rather too far and have taken Blake as furnishing a sort of criterion by which to read all the best of Romantic poetry.

During the past decade or so, Blake has had a very strong impact on modern poetry. Mr Louis Simpson recently wrote in the *New York Times* that 'Donne is out, Blake is in'. The most impressive evidence of this, perhaps, is Allen Ginsberg's vision in which Blake came to him and sang his songs, leading Ginsberg himself to compose and sing the *Songs of Innocence and of Experience* in public and on records. Ginsberg's knowledge of Blake is extensive and exact, and includes works other than the lyrics. Robert Duncan was deeply influenced by Blake and also knows him thoroughly. And Gary Snyder, though his own work shows no obvious Blakean influence, has remarked that 'Blake is father of us all'.

The sort of influence I have been talking of is to be sharply distinguished from the currency Blake has found among the psychedelic generation, in which he has been taken as the prophet of a mindless 'turning on' and letting go of everything but free floating images of the individual psyche. He would have been horrified.

Blake has become accessible and important as a poet, and even faddish. But he is not yet quite as accessible as he should be in the way he wanted to be known, as a poet-artist creating a composite art of words coupled with engraved designs. He himself published all but two of his works that were published, as prints with text and engraved designs which were hand coloured in water colour, and occasionally other media, by himself and in a few cases by his wife. The study of Blake until very recently has been concerned almost exclusively with the text alone, partly because of the difficulty in getting access to these works, each copy of which is at least in minor respects unique because the colouring altered the designs, but also partly because criticism did not have the tools with which to work on composite art. The text alone, of course, presented problems enough, and, since as an artist even in pictures that are not related to a text Blake is such a literary painter that art historians are often put off by him, it was possible to deal with one thing at a time and start with the text.

Materials for the study of composite art have become more readily available largely resulting from an extended programme of the Blake Trust, through the Trianon Press, which has produced hand coloured facsimiles of selected originals so faithfully reproducing the originals that the late Sir Geoffrey Keynes called them 'almost forgeries'. We were given the beginnings of iconographic study of Blake over a half century ago by Joseph Wicksteed, who taught us that the left hand is material and the right hand spiritual. But with the exception of studies by Jean Hagstrum, Kathleen Raine and an essay contest sponsored by David V. Erdman and John Grant which resulted in a collection of studies of Blake's work as composite art, or 'visionary forms dramatic', most examinations of the pictorial aspect of these works has consisted pretty much of mere description.[2]

It is not within the scope or purpose of this book to deal with Blake's work in its totality as text and design—or to attempt to formulate the sort of critical theory that would be needed for such an enterprise. Perhaps, in writing yet another book which concentrates on the text of Blake as abstracted from his own 'illuminated' pages, I am shrinking from the task that needs to be done and telling only half the story; but in an introductory book this seems unavoidable. While it will clearly be impossible to devote the attention to the engraved designs that they deserve, I will try to notice illustratively a few especially important designs in the course of the discussion of the poems.

But since Blake's composite art grows out of a life spent in practicing the arts of painting and poetry together—with perhaps some music as well—it would be appropriate to summarize if only briefly the facts of his biography.

William Blake was born 28 November 1757, to James Blake and Catherine Harmitage Blake, then about thirty-four and thirty-five, respectively.[3] He was the third of seven children, six boys and one girl, two boys dying in infancy. His oldest brother, James—who shared with him the powerful eidetic imagination enabling him to see visions but sharing little else—was four years his senior and inherited their father's hosiery shop when the father died. His next eldest brother, named John, died in infancy. After William there was born another brother named John in 1760—whom Blake identified as 'the evil one'—about whom little is known except that he joined the army and died; Richard, in 1762, who also died in infancy; Catherine, his only sister, in 1764, who survived all; and his favourite brother, Robert, in 1767, who prior to his death at nineteen seemed to be following in William's footsteps. Blake's parents were probably Baptists or at any rate dissenters, as is suggested by the burial of members of the family in Bunhill Fields, the dissenters' burying ground. William Butler Yeats and John Ellis, in the biographical and critical apparatus of their ambitious edition of Blake's works in 1893, gave currency to the idea that Blake's family were originally Irish and named O'Neill, but there is no evidence to support this. Even so, the myth dies hard, especially in Ireland.

Blake probably learned to read and write from his mother, for he attended no regular school, possibly because his parents wisely recognized that school was not quite an appropriate experience for him. For very early, at least at four, he began to show the visionary imagination that showed him God putting 'his head to the window', an experience which frightened him out of his wits, and later put angels among the haymakers, as well as filling a tree full of angels. He had a passion for drawing, and at the age of ten he was sent to a drawing school run by Henry Pars. He must have shown considerable promise, because there was talk of apprenticing him to some famous artist; but at William's own request he was apprenticed instead to an engraver, James Basire, because it cost less and was therefore more fair to the other children. This was a happy choice, because it furnished him with a craft by means of which he could support himself fairly congenially in the conventional world and also give form in the combination of poetry and design to less conventional ideas. Also by a lucky accident, because Blake did not get along with the newer apprentices, Basire sent him after two years to Westminster Abbey to make sketches for engravings commissioned by the Society of Antiquaries. In the statuary of the Abbey, he found a style of art that was to inform his work for the rest of his life. He seems to have spent most of five years in the Abbey making sketches. The Abbey of course was not the only artistic influence on him, for very early he had begun to buy prints, being encouraged and supported in this by his father.

During the period of his apprenticeship, between the ages of fourteen and twenty-one, and possibly even earlier, he had also begun to write poetry, prose poems, and dramas (never finished). Because he never attended a regular school, his reading was probably undirected, but there is no doubt that it was both extensive and intense, and included poetry of his age and of the renaissance. Most notably, it included the Bible and Milton, as well as Shakespeare and Chaucer. To judge from these early writings, which were presented as *Poetical Sketches* in 1783, Blake was as much a poetical prodigy as Alexander Pope. He certainly seemed to have a truly phenomenal ability in foreign languages, learning both French and Italian in a few weeks each, the latter when he was sixty-five in order to read Dante for the illustrations he was commissioned to execute.

His composition of poetry during the early period was accompanied, evidently, by musical composition in the form of melodies to which he is said to have sung his songs—which as a contemporary J. T. Smith, said were 'sometimes most singularly beautiful, and were noted down by musical professors'.[4] Whether he actually composed music for all his songs simultaneously with writing the words, as an early biographical sketch (by Cunningham) suggests, his lyrics are singable, as is shown by the very large number of musical settings of them by contemporary composers.

After he completed his apprenticeship, he studied for a while at the Royal Academy of Art and met there some of the leading artists of the time, including the famous Joshua Reynolds, whose *Discourses* he had read and did not like at all. Reynolds was pleasant but patronizing, advising him to work with 'less extravagance and more simplicity' and to improve his drawing, at which Blake was deeply offended and remained so. Blake had then, as always unshakably strong opinions, which he was glad to discuss gently with those who accepted them with respect but not so gently sometimes with those who put him down. If he felt he was being exhibited as a sort of freak who had visions, he was apt to make the most outrageous statements; but he would talk very patiently and sensibly with anyone willing to take seriously his visionary faculty—

which he felt anyone could cultivate if he wanted to. In 1780 he exhibited a water colour drawing at the Royal Academy, one of the few times he was to exhibit there because he did not like painting in oil, the regular medium for exhibitions, preferring tempera and water colour, as he told Reynolds.

Also in 1780 he had an experience which was accidental but memorable. While out walking on the evening of 6 June, he found himself swept up by a mob in the Gordon 'anti-popery' riots, on its way to burn Newgate and release the prisoners. Whether he was sympathetic with their cause or not (and he probably was) he had no choice but to run along in the front rank and witness the burning of the prison. The experience of suddenly and inadvertently participating in this sort of demonstration was memorable and frightening.

About this same time, at the age of twenty-three, he formed a lifelong friendship with other young artists, especially Henry Fuseli (the Swiss artist, Heinrich Füssli, who anglicized his name), George Cumberland, Thomas Stothard, and the sculptor John Flaxman. Sometimes he went sailing with Stothard and other friends. By 1782 his favourite brother Robert, ten years his junior and temperamentally close to William, was studying at the Royal Academy and was probably being helped by William.

Also in 1782 he 'kept company' for a time with a 'lively little girl', who evidently was not as serious about it as he, and when he complained that she had been strolling of an evening with another, she responded with a scornful look and said, 'Are you a fool?' which, says Blake, cured him of jealousy. Sometime after this he was visiting in Battersea and there met Catherine Boucher, daughter of a market-gardener, and asked her if she pitied him, to which she replied 'Yes', and he promptly said, 'Then I love you'.[5] It must have been love at first sight for her, for we are told she almost fainted when she first saw him. They were married in August 1782, when Blake was beginning to earn enough to support a wife. Because Catherine signed her name with an X in the church register of St Mary's, Battersea, it has been confidently assumed that she was illiterate and that her husband taught her to read and write; but, as G. E. Bentley has reported, signing with an X was not uncommon because 'writing was perhaps a difficult and precarious skill which it was thought best not to attempt in moments of emotional stress'.[6] In any event, Catherine, a beautiful woman four years younger than her husband, turned out to be the perfect exemplar of the help meet for a genius, learning to draw and colour some of the illuminated books, to print off engravings, and to share his visions. Her loyalty may be judged from a remark, when both were old, in response to a friend's observation that they were without soap: 'Mr Blake's skin don't dirt'. They never had any children.

At this same time Blake was being introduced to a wider social circle in the home of the bluestocking Mrs A. S. Mathew, with whom he became acquainted through his friend Flaxman. Harriet Mathew, the wife of the Rev. A. S. Mathew, brought to her home 'most of the literary and talented people of the day',[7] including musicians, and it was here that Blake first came to notice as a poet and singer of his own songs. Harriet Mathew and Flaxman, always eager to help his friend, prevailed upon the Rev. Mathew to help pay for the printing of the miscellany of works Blake had composed up to that time as *Poetical Sketches*, 1783. They were printed but not published in the ordinary sense of the term. The 'Advertisement', probably by A. S. Mathew, does, however, present them to 'a less partial public' than the one at the Mathews' home, who encouraged their printing to rescue them from oblivion; but evidently none were put out for sale, and Blake seems not to have been interested in promoting them. Part of the reason for this may be the apologetic preface, representing the collection as the work of a poetical primitive, 'the production of an untutored youth, commenced in his twelfth, and occasionally resumed by the author till his twentieth year', after which the author is said to have abandoned poetry in pursuit of another career. But, says the 'Advertisement', though they are full of 'irregularities and defects to be found on every page', the author's friends think they have enough 'poetic originality' to merit 'some respite from oblivion'.[8] Perhaps, in the perspective of the cultivated *salon* of his wife the Rev. Mathew did think of Blake's early poems as being interesting for their originality and novelty only, and no doubt his part in the publication was well intentioned. But it is hard to imagine Blake as very pleased to have his poetry passed off as little more than a curiosity. He had much too much confidence for that, and he was right to have it. It used to be thought that Blake's boisterous satire, *The Island in the Moon*, written in 1784 but neither published nor printed, was directed at Harriet Mathew's bluestocking *salon* because in it he pokes fun at various kinds of intellectuals—philosophers, scientists, antiquarians, etc.—but, as we shall see, he probably had another satiric object in mind.

In 1784 Blake's father died, probably leaving him a small inheritance which he invested in an artistic-commercial venture with James Parker, an apprentice with him at Basire's. The two began a print shop, which Blake later said was 'in those a rare bird', where the partners not only would sell the prints of others but would also produce their own. It was not a success and soon closed. But there were other gratifications. Blake's brother Robert was probably living with them, Blake exhibited two drawings at the Royal Academy, earning the accolade from the famous artist Romney that they 'rank with those of Michael Angelo'; and a certain John Hawkins was so impressed with Blake's work that he attempted to raise a subscription to send him to Italy and offered to pay most of his expenses himself. This never materialized. But in the spring of 1785 Blake exhibited four additional drawings.

In the winter of 1786 Robert, then nineteen, became fatally ill, and Blake attended him constantly, without sleep the last fortnight, then sleeping for three days. At the moment that Robert died, Blake saw, as Gilchrist puts it, 'the released spirit ascend heavenward through the matter-of-fact ceiling, "clapping its hands for joy" '.[9] Robert seems to have been more a son than a brother to him, certainly a kindred spirit. Robert is supposed to have revealed in a vision to William the process for producing his illuminated books, and Robert's notebook became a special source of imaginative stimulation, becoming William's own notebook, which contains drafts of many of his best known lyrics.[10]

In 1788 he tried out the process of illuminated printing, in which text and design were printed and then hand coloured, in three tiny tractates, *There Is No Natural Religion* I and II and *All Religions Are One*, which argue in a series of related but not rigorously consecutive aphorisms, with a conclusion at the end of each, for the poetic genius as the source of religion.

The following year marks the real beginning of Blake's production of printed illuminated texts with the appearance of *Songs of Innocence* and *The Book of Thel*, announcing on the title-pages that he was both 'author & printer'. The year 1789 is the year of publication, not composition, for two of the songs of *Innocence* appeared in *The Island in the Moon* in the MS of 1784, and it is likely that other songs were written in the intervening period. At this same time, Blake wrote a narrative poem, 'Tiriel', telling of the decline and death of an aged king of that name and involving a large fictional family. For 'Tiriel' he also made a series of drawings, but neither text nor designs were ever engraved, so the dating must remain uncertain, though a date of 1789 is generally accepted as being about right.[11]

Songs of Innocence are, of course, one half of a set of contrasting lyrics, the whole set being *Songs of Innocence and of Experience*, 'Shewing the Two Contrasting States of the Human Soul', and after *Songs of Experience* were engraved, in 1794, Blake never issued the first part of the set by itself. There is some evidence to suggest that from the outset he had in mind contrasting groups of lyrics. The development of the symbolic scheme underlying the lyrics, as we shall see later, seems to require a conception in which both Innocence and Experience exist as contrasts—or perhaps, as Northrop Frye says, as 'parodies' of each other. However that may be, it is clear that in these lyrics and in *Thel* as well as in 'Tiriel', Blake's visionary art in poetry has suddenly taken a sharp turn toward being systematized in the dialectical pairing of the two 'contrary states of the human soul'—from which is generated a complex third state that combines them—and in the development of poetic narratives that have the characteristics of myth. Looking back from the works of 1789, one can see these elements suggested in *Poetical Sketches*; but now we have a new voice.

We also have a new kind of art, the composite art of illuminated printing, in which etched designs literally intertwine with the text, reinforcing the rhythms of the poetry by undulating tendrils that often take the place of punctuation—in which Blake is notoriously casual, because he can afford to be on a plate where the lines are rhythmically modulated by other means. The pictures sometimes illustrate the text quite realistically but more often present parallel symbolic visions that, in a sense, comment on the text or greatly expand its meaning, playing contrapuntally against the words. In the period prior to *Songs of Innocence* and *Thel*, Blake had developed the arts of poetry and painting in parallel but had not directly connected them—except in the sense that, as a 'historical' painter, his visual art was literary. Poetry had been connected with music in *Poetical Sketches*, and may have continued to be after them. Blake's poetry is full of musical imagery in which even instrumentation is fully specified, and that great unfinished masterpiece, *The Four Zoas*, has many of the structural characteristics of a fantastic sort of opera, with its many arias, choruses, and ballets. With the exceptions of *Poetical Sketches*, which were published for him; *The French Revolution*, which got into type and a proof but no further; and the *Descriptive Catalogue* for his private exhibition in 1809, all his published works were issued in illuminated form.

Critics have offered a variety of interesting explanations for the sudden development of his art at this time and immediately after. I do not wish to minimize the possible importance of influences and sources. But tracing his sources is at best an uncertain business because of the fierce individuality of his mind. Without denying that, through his voracious and unusual reading and conversations with a variety of people, he came in contact with many ideas, for our present purpose it is perhaps sufficient to account for the mature voice of his 'prophetic' works—including the prophetic lyrics—by noticing that he was mature indeed, being thirty-two when *Songs of Innocence* were issued, and by suggesting that his invention of illuminated printing brought the two arts of poetry and painting together in a way that helped open the way for the development of the 'giant forms' of the mythic structures that were beginning to make their appearance in the works of 1789.

In *The Marriage of Heaven and Hell*, a strange work that is part satire on Swedenborg and part theoretical treatise on the epistemological and ontological doctrines essential to a radically visionary view of existence, Blake systematized his ideas in a different way. In 1788 he had become attracted to the writings of Emanuel Swedenborg, the Swedish scientist and religious visionary who recorded in 'memorable relations' conversations with angels and whose writings led to the founding of the 'New Church' which was to replace the 'Old'. The date of the founding of the New Church was 1757, the year of Blake's birth, and possibly this struck him as a significant correspondence. In 1789 he and Catherine signed their names to a statement at a conference of the New Church declaring that the signatories 'approve of the Theological Writings of Emanuel Swedenborg, believing that the Doctrines contained therein are genuine Truths, revealed from Heaven, and that the New Jerusalem Church ought to be established, distinct and separate from the Old Church'.[12] The meeting also passed thirty-two binding resolutions concerning doctrines and procedures which, presumably, the Blakes to some extent accepted. Fairly soon after that, however, Blake began to have some doubts concerning Swedenborg. He had found much to admire in *Divine Love and Wisdom* (1788), but was sharply critical of *Divine Providence* (1790), finding Swedenborg's predestinarianism totally unacceptable: 'Predestination after this Life is more Abominable than Calvins & Swedenborg is Such a Spiritual Predestinarian. . . .'[13]

There was long a tradition that Blake had been a Swedenborgian from youth, but this has now been clearly corrected. He had a brief fling with Swedenborgianism and found some things to admire, like the idea of 'correspondences', the appearance of the internal in the external but was finally disappointed, recording his disappointment in *The Marriage*, which shows the strong influence of the German shoemaker-theosophist, Jacob Boehme. Blake may have been attracted to Boehme partly through the illustrative diagrams of Andreas Freher, which he pronounced to be the equal of Michelangelo. In Boehme he found support for his idea of the 'contraries' that are immanent in all of life and organize being into a creative polar conflict. He had read Swedenborg's *Divine Love and Divine Wisdom* as expressing an idea consistent with his contraries, which are beyond good and evil, but in Swedenborg's later work found that the doctrines of the New Church were perpetuating those of the old one, in not only basing morality on the divisive categories of good and evil, which he viewed as destructive distortions of the contraries, but also in making good and evil unchangeable in the next world. In *The Marriage* he seems to turn normal morality upside down, defining 'Heaven' or Good as reason and 'Hell' or what is called Evil as creative energy and exalting it; but his main objective is to change man's perceptions, by the corruscating fires of satire, and show him that there are no Good and Evil, only the creative contraries 'necessary to Human existence', which must be understood and allowed to interact without hindrance from a morality that would set one half of existence against the other.

A reference on the third plate of *The Marriage* to the New Church's having begun thirty-three years earlier, or in 1757, suggests that this work was begun in 1790—and a marginal note by Blake himself in one copy confirms this—but it was probably not finished until 1792 or 1793, because 'A Song of Liberty', appended to it and making a political application of some of its principles, refers to historical events of that time on the continent, but especially in France. The next quarter of a century was to be the period of the revolution and of war with France, which brought with it a domestic repression of freedom that eventually touched Blake very directly when he was tried for sedition and assault on a soldier in 1804. He was judged innocent of the charges as stated, but the political allegory which can be seen in practically all his works, brilliantly analyzed by David V. Erdman, could have been seen as seditiously intended according to the standards of the 'gagging acts' of 1792. For Blake was a 'liberty boy', and a more consistent partisan of the revolution than Wordsworth or Coleridge, who came after 1796–7 to regard their earlier partisanship, to use Coleridge's words, as a 'squeaking baby trumpet of sedition'.[14]

Blake's first work to give clear partisan support to the revolution was a poem, this time without engravings, written for Joseph Johnson, the radical publisher for whom he had been making engravings off and on since 1780, and whose circle included such men as Thomas Paine and William Godwin. There is some uncertainty as to whether Blake was an intimate member of the group. The story that he saved Tom Paine from arrest by warning him may not, regrettably, be true, but he knew Paine and the others. *The French Revolution*, which gives a prophetic account of events in France between about 19–21 June and 15 July 1789, was 'thoroughly republican' even though written at a time when a constitutional monarchy 'was still the most probable eventuality for France'.[15] The poem was to be in seven books, of which only the first was set in type, and it was neither published nor entered at Stationers' Hall, existing only in a unique proof copy. Whether any more was written we do not know. The fear of reprisals was evidently beginning to close in, as Johnson chose not to publish Paine's *The Rights of Man* in the same year, either. In the future Blake was to remain no less radical than he had been but he would be much less explicit and open, confiding his thoughts to private writings and assimilating his politics to the cosmic myth he was developing—where, though his political expressions were not actionable in court, they broadened his 'democracy' to apocalyptic proportions, showing the American and French revolutions as concrete stages in the ultimate revolution that would completely change man's perception of reality and put society on an entirely new basis.

Blake continued engraving for Johnson, making engravings for Erasmus Darwin's *Botanic Garden*; for a publication venture of thirty large plates from Milton as painted chiefly by his friend Fuseli; and, perhaps most notable, contributing to Stuart and Revett's impressive *Antiquities of Athens*. A commission for engravings that had a direct effect on his own work was that for the illustrations to Captain John Gabriel Stedman's *Narrative of a five years' expedition, against the Revolted Negroes of Surinam, in Guiana, on the Wild Coast of South America*, after paintings by Stedman himself. These illustrations very directly influenced the engraved designs for Blake's *Visions of the Daughters of Albion*, issued in 1794, which includes, among other things, an attack on slavery.

In the meantime, he directed his attention again to a political subject and a revolution, this time to one that was over and done with, in an illuminated book, *America: A Prophecy*, issued in 1793. The subtitle does not mean that the work makes predictions, but that the American revolution is viewed from an imaginative and visionary point of view. The action in *America*, which was influenced by and in turn influenced the American Joel Barlow, takes place as it were on a very wide screen on both sides of the Atlantic and includes no bloodshed, only a sort of bacteriological warfare in which 'plagues' sent to America by 'Albion's Prince' are turned back on Albion's Prince to defeat him by the rushing together of the historical Americans' in spiritual solidarity. Making their first appearance in this work are two of the mythological characters who will have a central role in Blake's work for some time: Orc, who here is the spirit of revolution and freedom, and Urizen, the god of established religion and therefore of kings. As the myth grows, Orc and Urizen will be closely connected, embodying the principles of revolt and oppression, and later will undergo further development.

Also produced in 1793 was a work in line engraving of eighteen plates consisting of emblematic pictures with captions: *For Children: The Gates of Paradise*. The emblems were selected from a larger number drawn in Blake's Notebook, and the set was somewhat altered and expanded about 1818 and addressed 'To the Sexes', to include a text that says, 'Mutual Forgiveness of each Vice / Such are the Gates of Paradise', and, in comments related to the emblems, gives the keys to the gates. The prologue and an epilogue, the latter addressed to 'The Accuser who is the God of This World', develop the theme that orthodox religion worships a corporeal god, who, as prince of the corporeal world, is Satan, whatever he may be called.

Yet another work in illuminated printing on a prophetic-political theme produced this year was *Europe*, which might be thought of as a companion piece to *America*, though different and much more difficult. Where *America* had treated with expansive spatial imagery an event in the past that was complete, *Europe* views the present, in 1793, in terms of the eighteen hundred years since Christ's first coming. By applying to the revolutionary Orc an imitative allusion to Milton's *On the Morning of Christ's Nativity*, the poem suggests that a second coming can be seen in the political situation, with Christ appearing not in peace but with a sword.

In the meantime, in addition to being busily engaged with a career in engraving that seemed to be moving ahead quite well, Blake had also been writing the lyrics of *Songs of Experience*, often in Robert's notebook, where we find the drafts of his most famous of these lyrics, 'The Tyger', probably written in the fall of 1792 and early 1793. *Songs of Experience* (1794) were apparently never issued separately from *Songs of Innocence*, or at least no separate issues have survived, and of course, as noted, the two sets of lyrics were part of a symbolic scheme which included both. In fact, Blake conceived of the two sets as being so closely related that he switched some songs from the two sets back and forth, so that a lyric that was in one issue a song of Innocence could in another become a song of Experience. There was also no fixed order in the sets. *Songs of Innocence* were, of course, issued as a set prior to their companion lyrics, but Blake's conception of Innocence is complex and that complexity is reflected in different kinds, or, rather, different strata of lyrics.

The individual lyrics are certainly able to stand on their own as poems, but they are enriched by Blake's schematic framework, in which he had developed his moral philosophy—in the broader sense of that term—prior to his having begun to work out a more comprehensive and detailed view of human life (in its political and other aspects) in the huge fictional structure usually called his myth, where he can account fully for the dominance of Experience in human life. He never abandoned the idea of Innocence and Experience, continuing to issue the songs from time to time throughout the rest of his life, and defining Experience in a later work, the

Four Zoas. But the mythological characters like Orc and Urizen, who had appeared without much explanation in the political prophecies of 1793 and 1794, now absorbed his attention, and, in 1794 and 1795, he issued the works usually called 'the Lambeth books' because he produced them while living at 13 Hercules Buildings, Lambeth, where he lived from 1790 to 1800. These books are: in 1794, *The First Book of Urizen* (there was never to be more than one); in 1795, *The Book of Ahania*, *The Book of Los*, and *The Song of Los*, all in illuminated printing, in which the pictorial part of his composite art becomes more important than ever. *The Book of Urizen* contains several plates on which there is no text at all.

The Book of Urizen, the central narrative in this group of books, may be the 'Bible of Hell' which Blake had announced in *The Marriage*, for it tells the story of the Fall and ends with the departure of Urizen's children from Egypt, thus carrying a narrative which, though very different from the Bible, follows approximately the story of the Bible from Genesis to Exodus. Urizen, who was in *America* the 'god of kings', is here represented as abstract reason and materialism striving for a completely ordered and stable—and hence dead—universe organized by science and religion, and governed by law and the mystery of holiness. Urizen is the demi-urge in the sense that material creation comes into being as a consequence of his programme, which he develops in secret. But he does not actually create the material world himself, as we shall see later when we discuss this work in more detail. In this book Blake adds further detail to the relations between Urizen and Orc and associates Los, the 'prophetic spirit', with them. The other books in this group develop related aspects of the narrative and apply the events of the core narrative to the history of man.

In putting Urizen, Orc, and Los together in an organized relation-ship—with Ahania, Urizen's emanation, and Enitharmon, Los's emanation—Blake had developed his cast of symbolic-mythological characters to the point where he could now bring his whole mythic structure into total coherence by adding a fourth figure and making them all aspects of a total form of humanity in the giant Albion, whose emanation would be Jerusalem, both a totally organized female form and the city of God. He did this in a tremendous poem on which he worked from about 1795 until possibly 1808 but never finished, *Vala, or the Four Zoas.* The original title was *Vala*, and, as

H. M. Margoliouth showed, there was a poem based on this character. But Blake apparently got the idea of the four 'zoas' or aspects of Albion, each with an emanation or female counterpart, and changed the poem into a much larger narrative account of the Fall of man than was presented in *The Book of Urizen* and associated narratives, bringing the story around to the apocalypse. *Vala* was written on proof sheets for the illustrated edition of Edward Young's *Night Thoughts*, for which Blake designed the illustrations —over 500 of them, not all engraved and published—and Blake's poem followed Young's in being divided into 'nights' rather than chapters or books. In this work Blake's myth suddenly explodes. Though often confusing because it is unfinished, it is nevertheless one of the very greatest works of literature and an essential work for anyone who wants to know Blake. The ninth night, the apocalypse, bursts with incredible creative energy.

After the enormously productive period of 1793–5, Blake produced no more works of illuminated printing until the pair of great epics, *Milton* and *Jerusalem*, dated on their title pages 1804 but not actually printed then, probably not until after 1809 for *Milton*, the 'minor' epic, and much later for *Jerusalem*, the 'major' one. He was at work, however, on *Vala*, or *The Four Zoas*, as it was later titled, from about 1796 on, clearly conceiving text and some designs together at the outset, for the MS includes a number of drawings. He probably continued work on *The Four Zoas* until about the time that *Milton* was engraved and ready to be printed and a good deal of work had been done on *Jerusalem*. He was thus engaged in writing three huge epics at the same time. As was characteristic of him, he projected even huger ones: *Milton* was to be in twelve books instead of two, and *Jerusalem* was at one point to be in twenty-eight chapters rather than four—though perhaps the chapters would have been shorter. In 1804 he announced that he would once again display his 'Giant forms to the public', and he intended to display them on a stage to match, not wanting to continue with the smaller epic-like forms of the first half of his residence in Lambeth.

For almost fifteen years he was engaged in these huge works, first *The Four Zoas* and then the two major published works. But other projects and other events also intervened. One project was that of making designs for Edward Young's *Night Thoughts*, a poem on life, death, and immortality in nine 'nights', published with Young's text in a box in letterpress surrounded by Blake's designs. And he illustrated Gottfried Augustus Bürger's *Leonora*, as well as George Cumberland's *Thoughts on Outline* (1796). He also exhibited a painting, *The Last Supper*, at the Royal Academy. In 1799 he was commissioned for a painting by the Rev. Dr Trusler, who did not like it at all and charged Blake with being too much in the spirit world, which he found an odd complaint to come from a clergyman and said so in a letter.

His finances were not in good condition during this time, for he was not getting enough work. Since 1794 Thomas Butts had been steadily commissioning various kinds of works of art and often was his sole source of income, a worthy friend as well as a faithful patron despite his not having a large income. Then in 1800 another patron—or perhaps more accurately agent or manager— came actively into Blake's life in an episode that turned out to be crucial. This was William Hayley, the friend and biographer of Cowper and incredibly prolific writer of all manner of works, an indefatigable literary projector, who wanted to be to Blake a benefactor as he had tried to be to Cowper and others. Blake's epigrams about Hayley and the biographical strain in *Milton* have given Hayley a worse press among readers of Blake than he deserves. For he really did try to serve Blake as a benefactor and defended him against Lady Hesketh (a friend of Cowper's who thought Blake was unable to draw elephants and babies) and, most import-ant, defended him in court against a charge of sedition. Hayley clearly did not understand Blake's genius, regarding him as a 'gentle visionary . . . sublimely fanciful and kindly mild',[16] and it is possible that Blake never showed him any of the illuminated books, which could hardly be said to be merely 'fanciful', whether sublimely or not. Hayley knew Blake primarily as an artist and engraver, and invited him to move to the coastal village of Felpham, to live in a cottage near Hayley's own 'Marine Villa' with its turret, where Blake could improve his income by work com-missioned by Hayley (tempera paintings for his library of artistic and poetic worthies of all ages, for instance) and by other work promoted by Hayley. Blake was at first very enthusiastic about this new opportunity and wrote glowing letters about his prospects soon after moving to Felpham in 1800. With Hayley he was making good progress in the study of Greek and Hebrew and in portrait painting in miniature.

He stayed at Felpham for three years, full of hope at first but gradually growing restive with miniatures when his 'Giant forms' were not being developed, coming to feel eventually that Hayley was jealous of his ability, and suffering from the sea air. Mrs Blake especially suffered, developing a bad case of rheumatism which it took 'Mr Birch's Electrical Magic' in London to cure later. But in order to last three years, the experience could not have been as bad as Blake's epigrams suggest. Hayley was not a very perceptive man, no doubt, as is suggested by his writing a three-volume essay on Old Maids which of course outraged every old maid in England. But his intentions with Blake, except for possibly wanting to manage him rather as a theatrical or concert manager might, were unselfish. He was, in Blake's terms, a 'corporeal friend' certainly and he tried to be a 'spiritual' one as well. If he turned out to be a spiritual enemy, in the sense that he really did not understand anything but a most conventional imagination, he was that un-wittingly.

Before the Blakes left Felpham an event occurred of a shattering kind, one that perhaps in Blake's mind verified the correctness of his earlier decision not to speak out explicitly on political matters as he had begun to do in *The French Revolution*, some thirteen years earlier. He was charged by two soldiers, whom he physically ejected from his garden and compelled down the road by the elbows, with having uttered the seditious remarks, 'Damn the King' and 'all you Soldiers . . . are sold for Slaves', and saying that Buonaparte could take possession of England in an hour.[17] The soldiers were named Scholfield and Cock (both variously spelled) and were later to appear as accusers in *Jerusalem*. During an era of political repression such as had existed in England since 1792, and in time of war, such charges were dangerous, especially when made by soldiers, who as loyal and brave subjects are apt to have a special credibility. A verdict of guilty as charged could have resulted earlier in extended imprisonment or even hanging. There is no doubt that Blake had often damned the King explicitly—he had certainly done so obscurely in his poetry—and he clearly thought soldiers were sold as slaves. George Cumberland's son reported at a later time that Catherine Blake, who shared all her husband's opinions, once remarked that 'if this Country does go to War our K––g ought to loose [*sic*] his head'.[18] The evidence was not strong enough to make the charges stick, and Blake was probably technically innocent, whatever his private sentiments about kings and soldiers. He also had excellent legal counsel in a certain Samuel Rose, a friend of Hayley's, and good support from Hayley himself. Though the trial, 11 January 1804, was presided over by the Duke of Richmond, who was hostile partly because he disliked Hayley, Blake was found innocent, and the verdict was so pleasing to the crowd that 'the court was, in defiance of all decency, thrown into an uproar by their noisy exultations'.[19] Blake, though ably represented by counsel, could not help speaking out from time to time with a ringing 'false!' at the testimony, and years later a person who had been there remembered only his 'flashing eye',[20] which must have been impressive.

Thus the Felpham episode, which had ended in September 1803 when the Blakes moved to 17 South Molton Street in London, came to a dramatic conclusion. In the trial the Satanic 'accusers' who had figured in his myth became all too real to him in the persons of Scholfield and Cock. And, released now from the kindly if imaginatively limiting advice and help of Hayley—and from embarrassing money-making schemes like the engravings of animals for which Hayley had dashed off silly poetic fables—he could concentrate his energies without distraction on the big epics featuring the giant forms of Los, the other 'zoas', and the total giant form Albion, who encompassed them all. He immediately turned to *Milton* and *Jerusalem*, as the title pages show in being dated 1804. The experience at Felpham, which had finally turned out to be so alien to him, had nevertheless furnished matter for a major work on the imagination focusing on a great exemplar of the Poetic Imagination who, he felt, had been limited by a dominant system that was essentially alien to true imagination—Milton. And it also helped bring into focus more concretely a whole host of themes that he had been developing rather generally in *The Four Zoas*. He also began working on an epic that was no less comprehensive in scope but more sharply directed. Instead of a narrative of a dream in the mind of Albion, he now addressed the four chapters of his new work, *Jerusalem*, to four audiences: 'To the Public', 'To the Jews', 'To the Deists', and 'To the Christians'. The two works, dated 1804, were probably conceived as closely related. Northrop Frye has suggested that they are like a prelude and a fugue.

Blake had not yet abandoned *The Four Zoas*, for, though he was mining that work for material for the new ones, some manuscript additions to *The Four Zoas* come from the others. But the myth of the Fall and redemption of man in the dream of nine nights that he had been working with in a sort of operatic form could be assimilated to the more rigorous contrapuntal treatment in the two new works, and also made more concrete. The conception of the 'zoas', the four natures that are in every man and which must interact in a vital harmony for man to realize his divine potentiality for joy and wisdom, represented a tremendous breakthrough in Blake's moral philosophy. But, without completely abandoning this idea, Blake seemed to feel the need to bring his psychological ideas to a more practical level, and with Hayley lurking in the background of his mind, he turned his attention to developing a few characters who were subsidiary in *The Four Zoas* in formulating a notion of the 'three classes of men': 'the reprobate', 'the redeemed', and—called that ironically—'the elect', who are, respectively, the wrathful man of energy, the ordinary good man susceptible of being imposed upon, and the mild 'satanic' man who wants to impose his will on the elect and to whose ministrations the elect man is susceptible. Blake himself was a combination of reprobate and redeemed, and Hayley, certainly, without intending evil, became in this formulation rather satanic. But neither of these works was to be published, which is to say printed and coloured, for some years to come.

In the meantime, Blake continues his art, being commissioned by an engraver-publisher, Robert Cromek, to make drawings for an edition of Blair's *The Grave*, which he was also to engrave, as well as to paint an illustration for Chaucer's Canterbury Pilgrims, also to be engraved. Cromek, whom Blake called a 'cheating Knave', got another engraver to execute the Blair designs and commissioned another painter, Blake's friend Stothard, to produce a painting for the Canterbury Pilgrims. Blake was furious and discharged his wrath in epigrams, as he often did, but went on to complete the picture for Chaucer for himself and also made a huge engraving of it. He had produced other paintings, notably a large painting of the *Last Judgment*, expanding the engraving of the subject in *The Grave* for the Countess of Egremont. The painting is now lost, but we have a description of it by Blake in his fascinating *Descriptive Catalogue* for an exhibition of his works which he privately held in the rooms of his brother James, the hosier, in 1809. Here he also exhibited his *Chaucer*. A few people came, notably the diarist and collector of literary and artistic notables, Henry Crabb Robinson, who later visited Blake often and recorded some strange conversations. And Charles Lamb came and was appreciatively interested. But no one bought any pictures. Blake was and had been eking out a living with occasional engraving, such as illustrations for the *Iliad* (1805) after Flaxman, and from 1809 on the living became precarious indeed and the work not very rewarding. In 1815–16 he was drawing and engraving illustrations for Wedgwood's catalogue of pottery.

Blake sinks almost from sight for several years, until 1818, when the son of his long time friend George Cumberland introduced him to a young artist, John Linnell, then twenty-six. Quite suddenly Blake found himself loved and admired to adulation by Linnell's circle of friends. One group of them formed themselves into a kind of society called 'the Ancients' because of their conviction that ancient man and ancient values were superior to modern—anticipating the Pre-Raphaelite Brotherhood and going back even farther than they for inspiration. Blake became for them 'the interpreter', probably an allusion to the house of the interpreter in *Pilgrim's Progress*, where Christian calls for guidance on his journey. Linnell was particularly helpful in a practical way, getting him work and commissioning it himself to the extent of providing Blake with a small but steady income.

Among the group of friends was John Varley, the painter and astrologist and teacher of painting, a huge man so full of energy and enthusiasm that he said, 'If it were not for my troubles I should burst with joy'. Varley was responsible for Blake's drawings of the famous 'visionary heads', which came to wide public notice in 1833 through Alan Cunningham's account of Blake in *Lives of the Most Eminent British Painters, Sculptors, and Architects*, picked up widely in magazines in Britain and America. Blake's visionary faculty seemed to work especially well late at night, when he would draw for Varley the portraits of all kinds of historical and non-historical figures who 'sat' for him in his mind's eye as if they were physically present. In addition to people like Richard the Lion-hearted, Blake drew the sensational 'Ghost of a Flea', a humanoid creature holding a cup for blood, of which Varley published an engraving in his *Zodiacal Physiognomy*.

Through Linnell Blake participated in a project for which he made his only woodcuts, the *Pastorals of Virgil . . . Adapted for Schools*, edited by Dr Robert John Thornton, a physician and biologist, with translations by various hands. The seventeen woodcuts Blake made for the new edition of this collection illustrated the first eclogue, translated by Ambrose ('Namby-Pamby') Phillips (1675?–1749), the pastoral rival of Pope and author of such lines as, 'Dimply damsel, sweetly smiling'. The imaginative power of Blake's tiny woodcuts simply overwhelms the book, despite being ignorantly cut down for printing. They open out three-dimensionally, like little windows. Dr Thornton failed to appreciate them and was in process of having them re-engraved by slick professional woodcutters when he was persuaded to stop by James Ward and Sir Thomas Lawrence. Still not sure, he preserved all but three in their original form but added a note apologizing for their lack of skill. These woodcuts had a powerful influence on Blake's younger disciples. In 1821, the year of the publication of Thornton's *Virgil*, the Blakes moved to 3 Fountain Court, Strand, in two rooms in a house of Catherine's sister and her husband.

In 1822 Blake produced the last of his illuminated works, a little play, *The Ghost of Abel*, dedicated to Lord Byron as Elijah, 'crying in the wilderness', as from one prophetic visionary to another. The play was written in response to Byron's recently published *Cain*, in which Cain, his sacrifice of vegetables being rejected by Jehovah in favour of Abel's sacrifice of burnt animal flesh, strikes Abel with a brand, killing him, and leaves to wander remorsefully in a world in which death had entered through his act. Blake's playlet makes the point that there was a satanic element in Abel's religion, as is suggested by his Ghost arising and calling for blood revenge and then sinking into a grave and rising again as Satan with a kingly 'Crown and a Spear', prince of this world. But in the true 'Visions of Jehovah', which Byron had missed, the Lamb comes in atonement and 'forgiveness of sins', and Satan himself will subdue and annihilate his satanic character. There is no evidence that Byron knew of this work.

Linnell's assistance to Blake, having led to the great woodcuts of the *Virgil* in 1821, also brought about the famous engraved iconographic exegesis of the Book of Job in the Job engravings, commissioned in 1823 by Linnell, and made from drawings of an earlier date for Butts. To many people these are Blake's masterpiece and they have been widely reproduced. Linnell shortly after commissioned a set of engravings illustrating Dante, for which Blake learned Italian so that he could read the original, and produced over a hundred marvellous water colour drawings from which to make engravings which do not merely illustrate, but comment on the text. And in 1825 he was engaged in water colour illustrations to Bunyan's *Pilgrim's Progress*. He was sixty-eight years old, and not in good health, suffering from stomach pains and intense shivering.

There was no lasting improvement in his health; evidently he was suffering from gallstones. The shivering fits continued, though he also continued to work. Finally, on 12 August 1827, he died, at six in the evening. He had been working that day colouring a print on the frontispiece to *Europe*, better known as 'The Ancient of Days', and had made a pencil sketch of Catherine. As death approached, he sang songs which he said were 'not mine' but came from another world. He had been indifferent as to where he would be buried, suggesting Bunhill where his family were. But oddly enough for a man who all his life had attacked the religious establishment he did request the Church of England service. He was lowered into an unmarked grave on 17 August. Through the efforts of Herbert Jenkins, the grave has been located and is now marked.

Catherine moved into John Linnell's home for a year and then became housekeeper to Fredrick Tatham, one of the young men attached to Blake. She helped her income from sale of his works and even returned a gift of £100 from Princess Sophia on the grounds that others needed it more.[21] She died 18 October 1831.

The works of Blake which Catherine possessed went to Tatham, who rather capitalized on them; worse, he destroyed some of Blake's papers, possibly some complete works that were mentioned and have not been found. In later years, some of those who had been disciples during the 1820s, having grown more conservative and orthodox with age, recalled Blake's heterodox opinions rather unsympathetically, and Tatham was among them. It may be that the destruction attributed to him has been exaggerated; and it was no doubt done to protect Blake from charges of heresy.

Blake's religion needs no defence, and, in any event, he expressed it in everything he did or said, so censorship was futile unless the whole record of the man could be wiped out. The complete contemporary record has only recently been compiled, by Professor G. E. Bentley Jr, and there are over six hundred pages of it. We

B

see in it, of course, the eccentric Blake of ancedote. But we also see the man who was a good deal in society, and who was taken seriously as a fine engraver and artist. Above all we see a man who, in Samuel Palmer's phrase, was that rarest of persons, one completely 'without a mask'.[22]

2 | *Poetical Sketches* and other early works

The collection called *Poetical Sketches* was printed, though not published, in 1783 at the initiation of John Flaxman and Harriet Mathew, with an anonymous apologetic preface. It was Blake's first work to get beyond MS. The title is apt enough, for the collection of unbound and uncut sheets contains a poetical miscellany of four poems on the seasons, two on times of the day, two ballads, seven songs, three miscellaneous poems, a 'War Song to Englishmen', a fragment of a drama, prologues to two more, and three works in poetic prose.[1] These pieces are his most nearly conventional work, including the traditional 'Imitation of Spenser' which every young poet of the period had to try, and others showing the influence of the Renaissance and the eighteenth century. But influences—let alone sources—have a rather bad time of it in Blake's work, even in these early pieces, because what comes through is the all but overwhelming individuality and originality of his voice. The 'Imitation of Spenser', so titled, is one that Spenser might not have immediately recognized as being that, except for the fact that some of the stanzas end with an Alexandrine. The poem is an extended invocation of Apollo, Mercury, and Pallas Athena for help in writing poetry of sense, not 'tinkling sounds', that 'round the circle of the world wou'd fly!' Anticipations of the prophetic voice of the bard are heard even here.

Blake's sounds in these poems are anything but 'tinkling'. The writer of the preface to the collection well might apologize for irregularities, because, from the point of view of regular verse, there are many. But Blake had no interest in regular metres unless they served the musical effects he wanted, and he had the confidence to trust his own ear as to what these should be. As a result, normal accentual scansion of the kind restricted to two degrees of accent is often not a very effective means for the analysis of the music of his verse. For the effect of music indeed, in the ordinary sense of the term, is very strong, and what seems awkward and metrically irregular sometimes turns out to make very good rhythmical sense if it is heard as being sung. He combines strong accentual rhythms with quantitative ones and also seems to write verses which imply considerably greater variations in tempo than usually appear when verse is read in the normal way. There was some quite reliable contemporary testimony that he sang his songs, especially those included in *Poetical Sketches*, to melodies of his own invention and some evidence that he continued the practice in some later works, conceiving melodies along with the poems, as he probably conceived designs along with the texts. Blake's melodies, which J. T. Smith said were so good that they were written down by 'musical professors',[2] have not survived, but it is valid to try to infer from the rhythms of the text the kinds of musical rhythms to which the words might have been sung.

'Mad Song' in this set is from an ordinary metrical point of view quite irregular but quickly comes into focus in imagined singing. The first verse goes:

> The wild winds weep,
>   And the night is a-cold;
> Come hither, Sleep,
>   And my griefs infold;
> But lo! the morning peeps
>   Over the eastern steeps,
> And the rustling birds of dawn
> The earth do scorn.

Musical metrics, being quantitative and arithmetically subdivisible, quantify the rhythms in a way in which speech rhythms would not, so the poem would not be read quite the way it would be sung. Musical and verbal rhythms pull against each other, as it were, to create a rhythmical tension, and I am not suggesting that the poem be read in quite the same way it would be sung with a tune, for that would be to chant it. Nevertheless, if even in reading the words by themselves we hear a possible musical rhythm along with the verbal rhythm, the verbal rhythm takes on a pattern which smooths out the apparent irregularities. In a musical setting, 'The' in the first line becomes an up-beat, and 'weep' is probably held longer than 'wild' and 'winds' but only long enough to allow for another up-beat on 'And the' in the next line. Musical-metrical notation of the first four lines of the stanza might be as follows:

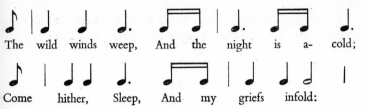

But here a rhythmic change occurs to a triple motion because the beat is subdivided into three, and it might be notated thus:

The last line seems to return to the duple rhythm of the first four, though it could be notated in triple if the last syllable, 'scorn', were held twice as long as 'earth' and 'do'.

If the poem is read with musical rhythms in mind, the contrasting sections of duple and triple rhythms are heightened because the movement in the triple section naturally picks up, and there will be less tendency to slight the strong accents on the last three syllables of the last line. As an experiment, harpsichordist Ruth Nurmi, long familiar with Blake and also very familiar with the musical idiom that he would have been brought up in, made an attempt to work through the text to not only musical rhythms but melodies like those which she imagined he might have thought of, assuming that, though he was not schooled in music, some principles of setting a musical text would naturally have occurred to him—such as rising intervals for the morning and the sky and perhaps intensification of an important word by an accidental. It is likely that Blake's tunes were strophic, the same tune for each stanza; but some songs like 'Mad Song' may not have been, if Ruth Nurmi's experiment is any indication, for she strongly felt the need for different melodic treatment of the second and third verses.

Another of the songs whose rhythm might be clarified by considering it as possibly being sung is 'Memory, hither come'.

> Memory, hither come,
>   And tune your merry notes;
> And, while upon the wind
>   Your music floats,
> I'll pore upon the stream,
> Where sighing lovers dream,
> And fish for fancies as they pass
> Within the watery glass.
>
> I'll drink of the clear stream,
>   And hear the linnet's song;
> And there I'll lie and dream
>   The day along:
> And, when night comes, I'll go
>   To places fit for woe;
> Walking along the darken'd valley,
>   With silent Melancholy.

These lines do not easily scan by syllables; they scan more easily by stresses. But thinking of them in relation to the stresses as reflecting musical beats makes reading even easier. The first three lines of each stanza have three beats, followed by a two-beat line (with an up-beat). Then follow two three-beat lines and one of four, ending with a line of three beats. The first lines of the two stanzas are rhythmically consistent if thought of musically, but they are very different in ordinary syllabic scansion, in which the first line would be scanned /∪∪/∪/ and the second ∪/∪∪// . Musical rhythm would give the same quantity to 'hither' and 'clear', with 'hither' being notated ♩ ♩ and 'clear' being notated ♩ . It seems to me that the two-beat lines, 'Your music floats' and 'The day along', might in singing have the same quantity as the prevailing lines of three beats but be stretched out in notes that are held longer, to produce a rhythm tension between verbal and musical rhythms and hence a sort of marking of the musical phrase, in the middle of the stanza.

In suggesting that these songs in *Poetical Sketches* are helped by considering them in relation to musical as distinguished from poetic rhythms, I do not intend to minimize Blake's originality as a poetic metricist. But since the poems are songs, and we know that Blake himself sang them, it seems reasonable to think of them in their musical connection. They can, of course, be scanned without any reference to music, in terms of the sort of accentual verse that Coleridge thought he was inventing in *Christabel*, and that kind of scansion is consistent with musical rhythm, or almost so. But it seems to me that the rhythms of these songs make even better sense if thought of in relation to music.

Another interest makes itself felt in the group of four poems on the seasons, for in these there is an anticipation of the cyclical patterns that will later inform Blake's myth. These lyrics have a technical interest too—and possibly also had a musical connection. Formally they are quite remarkable in giving something of the effect of poetic structural recurrence that usually is accomplished by rhyme patterns in stanzas *without* rhyme. Grammar and the stanza provide the structural rhythm here, each stanza being one sentence. There is also a structural pattern to the poems as a cycle— which is how they should be read—for the opening and closing poems are four stanzas of four lines each, and the middle poems are both three stanzas of six lines each.

Blake humanizes the seasons but invests his personifications with much greater intensity of character and sharpness of outline than is found in the personifications of abstraction in most poetry of the period. Spring comes as a lover with 'dewy locks' to a virgin 'lovesick' land. Summer is a hot ruddy youth, full of strength and energy, who is invited to tarry in the land. Autumn, a more mature figure, is a jolly singer who sings a song of fruitfulness and then departs. In 'To Winter' everything changes. The speaker of this poem addresses Winter, as he had the other seasonal figures, but is ignored and goes on to describe what Winter does. He had asked Winter to 'bar thine adamantine doors' and not shake 'thy roofs, / Nor bend thy pillars with thine iron car'—but to no avail:

> He hears me not, but o'er the yawning deep
> Rides heavy; his storms are unchain'd; sheathed
> In ribbed steel, I dare not lift mine eyes,
> For he hath rear'd his sceptre o'er the world.

> Lo! now the direful monster, whose skin clings
> To his strong bones, strides o'er the groaning rocks:
> He withers all in silence, and his hand
> Unclothes the earth, and freezes up frail life.

Where Spring, Summer, and Autumn had been agents of life
bringing fulfilment and fruitfulness to the earth, Winter reigns over
the earth as over a kingdom of death. Instead of remaining, as the
speaker asks him to do, in the north where he had built his 'dark /
Deep-founded habitation', he withers all—until heaven smiles once
more and 'the monster / Is driv'n yelling to his caves beneath mount
Hecla'.

There is in the cycle of seasons in these poems rather more than
a normal celebration of the natural cycle, partly because of the
vividness of all the persons but especially of Winter. Echoes of
James Thomson's picture of winter from *The Seasons* are heard in
the last stanza of Blake's poem, but Blake's Winter is a monster-
king ruling a deathful land and he takes on some of the characteristics that we shall see later in the ruler who identifies himself with
the North, Urizen, as the hot ruddy summer seems rather like the
energetic Orc. And Spring comes as a sexual redeemer. It is not
safe to apply Blake's later myth fully to earlier work; but even
in these poems some of the characteristics of his mythical figures
were taking shape. The emphasis in the seasons poems of *Poetical
Sketches* is not so much on nature as on the redemption of human
life.

A parallel cycle is the diurnal one in the pair of lyrics, 'To the
Evening Star' and 'To Morning'. Again the imagery is sexual, and
again a descent occurs to a malevolent state, in the night. The
Evening Star is addressed as 'fair-hair'd angel of the evening' and
asked to light the 'bright torch of love'. But 'Soon, full soon, /
Dost thou withdraw; then the wolf rages wide, / And the lion
glares thro' the dun forest'. The dew that was thought to come
with the Evening Star protects the flocks, until Morning comes,
personified in the companion poem as 'O holy virgin! clad in
purest white', to awake the dawn and salute the sun. In Blake's
later symbolism stars come to be associated with oppression and
virgins with a self-centred love, but not, fortunately, in this lovely
pair of poems.

The two verse narratives in *Poetical Sketches*, 'Fair Elenor', and
'Gwin, King of Norway', tell very different stories. 'Fair Elenor'

is a gothic verse narrative of gruesome horror in which the Lady
Elenor is given a wet napkin containing the bloody head of her
lord, murdered by an evil duke. When she gets it home, the napkin
unfolds itself revealing the head, which speaks to her. She kisses it,
hugs it to her breast, and dies. Other than the gruesomeness of the
story, the most noteworthy things in the poem are her lamentation
of her lord—who is compared in a series of similes to a flower, a
star, the dawn, and finally to a tree now cut down in whose leaves
'the breath of heaven dwelt'—and Blake's vital and metonymic
imagery, in which the bell sounding the hour shakes the tower,
groans are heard in the halls, and the vaults of the dead sigh.

A severed head, actually a split one, is also featured in 'Gwin,
King of Norway', but not for the chills of horror and romance.
'Gwin' opens with the formula of a ballad that teaches a lesson,
addressed to kings: 'Come, Kings, and listen to my song. . . .'
And the lesson it teaches is that kings who oppress their people
economically are going to be overthrown by popular armies of
husbandmen who will not be intimidated by fear of death in a war
with professional soldiers, and who will find a champion to lead
them, like the giant 'Gordred' of this tale. The tale owes the name
of its people's champion to Chatterton, but its burden, as Erdman
has pointed out, is probably related to Blake's attitude toward the
American revolution, which he was to celebrate a decade later
much less bloodily in *America: A Prophecy*.[3] Gwin is a mythical
king, and Norway is probably meant to specify the Scandinavian
country symbolically only in its northernness. But the economic
situation depicted is real enough:

> The Nobles of the land did feed
>   Upon the hungry Poor;
> They tear the poor man's lamb, and drive
>   The needy from their door!

Gordred, who has been sleeping in a cave, rouses himself and
'shook the hills, and in the clouds / The troubl'd banners wave', as
an army suddenly forms. Gwin calls his chiefs and prepares for
war, and he personally slays many of the shepherds and husbandmen
of the revolutionary forces, until

> The god of war is drunk with blood;
>   The earth doth faint and fail;

> The stench of blood makes sick the heav'ns;
> Ghosts glut the throat of hell!

But finally the giant Gordred and Gwin meet, 'like blazing comets in the sky', and the revolutionary giant divides Gwin's head 'from the brow unto the breast'. The nobles flee or are killed. This, of course, was written some time before 1783, before Louis XVI's head had been cut off by the instrument perfected (but not invented) by Dr Guillotine. A few years later, as Blake himself was to conclude, it would not have been wise to publish so explicit an *exemplum* even though set obscurely in Norway at some mythological time. And Blake was not to be so explicitly bloody in his poetry again. The gigantic Gordred is a kind of revolutionary spirit, but he is also, much more, a military champion, and so differs significantly from the Orc of the political prophecies.

It is a big step to take from this account of revolution to what seems, on the surface, to be a jingoistic celebration of a war of kingly conquest in the fragment of a play in six scenes, *King Edward the Third*; but many critics have been willing to take it. The situation of Edward in 1346 before the Battle of Crécy is somewhat parallel to that of Henry V before the Battle of Agincourt, and Blake's dramatic fragment owes something to Shakespeare's play of Henry, as well as to other plays of Shakespeare. But Blake's king and nobles in their speeches before the battle protest far too much about their cause of 'liberty'—whatever that could mean in this context—and exalt the glories of war for its own sake to overcome their nervous fear. The rhetoric is jingoistic, with a vengeance. But it cannot be taken at face value unless Blake is regarded as one of the most inept Shakespearean imitators in literature. The play is ironic, a satire on kingly war by exaggeration and parody, as is suddenly clear, if it was not at the outset, with the introduction of the character of William, Sir Thomas Dagworth's Man, who makes apparently disingenuous remarks that 'thrust the question home' and show that the whole business is concerned with immoral ambition for conquest and therefore can have little to do with liberty in any form. The divinity prayed to in the king's opening speech is clearly the 'god of war' described in 'Gwin, King of Norway', and the 'glory' constantly mentioned in the speeches is equated with bloodshed.

This dramatic fragment can be seen to have a rather deeper

irony if it is considered as saying something about events of Blake's own time, in the impending war with France in 1778. This contemporary political allegory is rather complicated, and its richness would be spoiled by an attempt at summary. It has been thoroughly examined by Professor Erdman. I might note in passing that in 1348, two years after Crécy, came the Black Plague, which swept Europe, and Blake connected pestilence and war. In 1784 he exhibited a design, *War unchained by an Angel—Fire, Pestilence, and Famine following* and another, *A Breach in a City —The Morning after a Battle*, showing a gruesome scene of death and devastation with no hint of 'glory' in it. Some of the imagery in the dramatic fragment hints at contagion and infection.

Blake had drawn Edward III for the Basire engraving in *Gough's Sepulchral Monuments*, and he later drew at least one visionary portrait, questioning him about 'the butcheries of which he was guilty in the flesh'. It is extremely unlikely that, as Professor Damon has suggested in his *Blake Dictionary*, 'Later, Blake changed his mind about Edward' after having glorified him in the play.[4]

King Edward the Third ends with a minstrel's song, though more than one was mentioned. Professor Erdman plausibly suggests that 'A War Song to Englishmen', printed a little later in *Poetical Sketches*, really belongs with the play, where it does fit thematically.[5]

Poetical Sketches concludes with three prose-poems, 'The Couch of Death', 'Contemplation', and 'Samson', showing the influences of Chatterton, Ossian, the Bible, Milton, and others. The first of these is a meditation at evening 'when Nature takes her repose', and recalls an old story of a dying youth attended by his mother and sister. The youth is conscious of sin and cannot reach out to God, but the mother shares his sin, and suddenly the youth dies and the imagery shifts to a scene of a traveller under an oak who 'eyes the distant country with joy!' An angel chorus with 'stringed sounds' is heard, and the youth 'breathes out his soul with joy into eternity'. This little piece is in prose that is rhythmically cadenced but not metrical. The slight narrative is heavily ornamented with similes, which produce some of the rhythmical effects. The mourning mother and sister are first 'like lilies', then 'like reeds bending over a lake' at evening. The speeches are orchestrated with imagery. The youth's voice was 'low as the whisperings of woods', and his mother's 'like the sound of a broken pipe'. Then his is 'like a voice heard from a sepulchre', and 'as the voice of an omen' and 'as the voice of the Angel of Death', as he despairs between 'the sinful world and eternity'. But his mother's voice suddenly changes and becomes 'like the bubbling waters of the brook' as she seeks to liberate the 'Voice that dwellest in [her] breast' to share his sin. The sighs of the mother and sister then come 'like rolling waves, upon a desert shore'. But now the imagery changes from sound to sight, as the youth becomes 'like a cloud tossed by the winds, till the sun shine, and the drops of rain glisten, the yellow harvest breaths, and the thankful eyes of the villagers are turned up in smiles'. The scene shifts to the pictorial image of the traveller under an oak viewing the country with joy—which might well be a drawing. And then the imagery returns to sound, but now to the musical sound of a chorus of angels with string orchestra.

The imagery of this piece tells a story of redemption, not merely that of the youth himself but of nature, which makes the villagers thankful. And we see here also an instance of the 'forgiveness of sins', which Blake saw as the great moral imperative for man supremely exemplified in Jesus. It seems to come about here when the mother takes on the sin of the son. And there is also in this early piece an apocalyptic conclusion with the angelic chorus that will be typical of the longer prophecies.

'Contemplation', the second of the prose pieces, is a dialogue between the poet and Contemplation, who urges him to find happiness by escaping to nature, and he replies, 'I am wrapped in mortality, my flesh is a prison, my bones the bars of death'. Such escape is not for him.

Finally, there is 'Samson', a sort of brief prose epic, with the traditional machinery of the statement of the subject and the invocation of the muse of 'Truth'. The narrative concentrates on Dalila's psychological torture of Samson by her feminine wiles and the perverseness which Blake will later associate with the 'female will'. And it also includes an account of the coming of Samson as foretold, as a deliverer.

Poetical Sketches are juvenilia, but, unlike most juvenilia, they let us hear Blake's own authentic voice. They reflect, as Professor Lowery has shown, a variety of influences, but Blake is not as indebted to his models as young poets usually are. He wrote lyrics called 'songs' as the Elizabethan and Caroline poets did, but they are different, showing technical developments in rhythms which were made possible by the typical Blakean confidence in his own ear as well as by his singing them himself. Had he continued to produce work of the kind in *Poetical Sketches*, and bring it to public notice by ordinary publication, he would have been at least a substantial minor poet speaking in a rather different voice from others of the time. But, if these works are reconsidered from the perspective of the illuminated books, they have a peculiar interest not only because they are the juvenilia of a major poet-artist but because we can see in them anticipations of elements that will appear in the prodigious imaginative structure of Blake's 'visionary forms dramatic' in the works to come.

The year after *Poetical Sketches* was printed, and Blake had entered into partnership with James Parker in the print shop hoping for financial success, he wrote an exuberant narrative—actually a sort of play with interpersed narrative—about a group of characters living on an island in the moon. It was long thought to be a satire on the set attending the literary and artistic *salon* of Harriet Mathew, written in pique because of the apologetic preface with which *Poetical Sketches* was printed. But it has been hard to identify the characters with those frequenting the Mathew evenings, and, if it is satire, it was not written in pique.

'The Island in the Moon', as editors have agreed to call it, is set, mostly, in the home of 'three Philosophers' named 'Suction, the Epicurean, Quid the Cynic, & Sipsop, the Pythagorean,' and the action involves conversations and musical entertainments with them and other characters with names like 'Etruscan Column the Antiquarian', 'Inflammable Gass the Windfinder', 'Obtuse Angle', 'Tilly Lally the Siptippidist', 'Aradobo, the dean of Morocco', 'Miss Gittipin', 'Mrs Nannicantipot', 'Gibble Gabble', and so on. As the names suggest, the characters represent people of various kinds of scientific and other endeavours and intellectual orientations. Blake himself, it is generally agreed, is Quid the Cynic—in the original philosophical sense of the term, a man who tries to be as independent as possible of external circumstances, not in the modern sense of the word, one who holds that everyone is motivated by selfishness. Other characters are harder to identify with certainty, but Suction is probably Robert Blake; Etruscan Column, Thomas Astle; Obtuse Angle, James Parker, Blake's partner; Steelyard, John Flaxman; and Inflammable Gass possibly Joseph Priestley, though there is good evidence to suggest a sort of scientific conjuror,

Gustavus Katterfelto.[6] The women are harder to identify. References in the conversations are made to additional characters whose identification is quite firm, including Dr John Hunter, the surgeon and print-collector ('Jack Tearguts'); and Richard Cosway, once a drawing instructor at Pars' school but later an extremely successful painter of miniatures and friend of the Prince of Wales. The conversations touch on Voltaire by name and, scatologically, on Dr Johnson.

Blake's fragment of a drama, *King Edward the Third*, can be thought of as satire of the ironic kind in which the object of the satire is represented as it might be by a proponent but with just enough exaggeration to let it be seen for what it is. Satire of this kind can be misunderstood, as Defoe had occasion to discover when he was pilloried for *The Shortest Way for Dissenters*, and as can be seen in some critics' attributing jingoistic attitudes to Blake.

'The Island in the Moon' is hard to characterize briefly because it is such a strange mixture, containing elements that range from musical comedy of a Gilbert and Sullivan kind to Swiftean satire and the comedy of the absurd. It has puzzled commentators. Recently Martha England has put 'The Island' in wholly new perspective by showing its probable connection with the improvisatory theatrical satires at the Haymarket by the master mimic and parodist, Samuel Foote, whose biting but extremely funny stage foolery resembles what goes on in 'The Island'.[7]

'The Island' is a variety show, theatrical in character—as is suggested by its having been staged at least twice. As such it grows out of the working assumption of comedy of the absurd, that the ordinary conventions of language and of action are suspended in the world of an absurd analogue to reality, with some of the uninhibited logic of a dream. Some of its language resembles the verbal play of Groucho Marx or Ionesco or Lewis Carroll: 'I think', says the foolish Aradobo, 'dean of Morocco'—a bookseller, 'in the first place that Chatterton was clever at Fissic Follogy, Pistinology, Aridology, Arography, Transmography Phizography, Hogamy Hatomy, & hall that but in the first place he eat wery little wickly that is he slept very little which he brought into a consumsion, & what was that that he took Fissic or somethink & so died.'

If we had no idea that some of the people represented in 'The

Island' were dear to Blake, his brother Robert for instance, and if he were not in it himself as Quid the Cynic, it would be possible to think of it as a nightmare rather than having the dream logic of the absurd. It does shift to some rather gruesome matters, like the description of John Hunter's surgery without anaesthetic ('hell Swear at them & keep them down with his fist & tell them that hell scrape their bones if they dont lay still & be quiet') or the reference to the screams of a 'woman having her cancer cut', and Quid sings a song attacking surgery. There is a good deal of strong irony in other songs. But that part of the satire which represents the characters of the social set engaged in intellectual discussions, which often begin and end with exuberant judgments that the subject is a 'sneaking knave' or a fool, is in its boisterous absurdity a celebration of the community of the group rather than an attack on its members. Its satiric caricatures are not vicious but affectionate, done in raucous fun.

Starting out in prose, in speeches connected by slight amount of narrative, in which the three 'philosophers' Suction, Sipsop, and Quid and others begin quarrelling about Voltaire, 'The Island' quickly turns into a musical show. It contains twenty songs indicated as being actually sung, not recited (one is specifically said to be recited). Half of them are sung at a drunken party at the philosophers' house, and seven more at 'another merry meeting at the house of Steelyard the Lawgiver'. All but Inflammable Gass the Windfinder and Etruscan Column the Antiquarian, among the major characters, sing a song or two, but Quid gives himself at least five of them to sing.

Most of the real satiric irony is in the songs. One of Quid's songs, 'When old corruption', is about surgery, in which surgery is born of the union of Corruption and flesh and then couples with a dead woman to bring forth scurvy and spotted fever. Steelyard the Lawgiver sings a song celebrating the charity of rich mayors and aldermen who give to the poor, apparently unconscious of any irony. And Obtuse Angle, or possibly Quid, sings a song characterizing matrimony as a golden cage. Dr Johnson is scatologically ridiculed in a parody of Collins' 'Ode to Evening', in which he is invited by Scipio Africanus to 'Lift up my Roman Petticoatt / And kiss my Roman Anus'. And the financial success of the Handel festival of 1784 is mocked in a song sung by the stupid amiable Scopprell.

In the midst of all these songs, Blake suddenly inserts three of a very different character and quality, which will later appear in *Songs of Innocence*: 'Holy Thursday', 'Nurse's Song', and 'The Little Boy Lost', sung, respectively, by Obtuse Angle, Mrs Nannicantipot (as her grandmother's song), and Quid (who, the MS shows, debated whom to give the song to before taking it himself). These are followed by a song about Joe and Bill in a controversy over bowling a ball into a 'turd', a sharply realistic contrast to the symbolic children of *Innocence*. Then comes a sad little song of a girl fading away in the sorrow of unrequited love to merge with nature, in a faint anticipation of the evanescent Thel.

What melodies Blake may have had in mind for the songs we do not know. We may get a scrap of Blakean music from the solfege syllables included in Scopprell's song on the Handel festival, 'Fa me la sol La me fa sol', which notated are:

And perhaps we can attach one of the songs to music in the last one of the piece, which is sung in response to a request for Handel's 'Waterpiece'. With a little metrical manipulation and repetition, the words can be sung to the music of the bourrée of the second suit in *Watermusic* (also called 'Air' or the seventeenth movement in other arrangements). The first part of the tune is:

And the words begin:

> A crowned king,
> On a white horse sitting
> With his trumpets sounding
> And Banners flying. . . .

After some missing leaves in the MS, the piece concludes with a conversation between Quid and an uncomprehending lady—not Mrs Blake—in which he plans his works for the future in illuminated printing, 'all the writing Engraved instead of Printed & at every other leaf a high finished print all in three Volumes folio', to be sold at 'a hundred pounds a piece'. At the very end Obtuse Angle enters; but the work breaks off.

3 | Early works in 'Illuminated Printing'

Quid–Blake's scheme for illuminated printing mentioned on the last leaf of the MS for 'The Island in the Moon' was to consist of having 'the writing Engraved instead of Printed & at every other leaf a high finished print all in three Volumes folio', he adds grandiloquently, and he would 'sell them at a hundred pounds a piece'. Illuminated printing as he finally devised it—with a hint from his brother Robert in a vision after his death in 1787—was to be quite different. Both the text and designs were usually on the same plate, though some works contain plates with no text. And the plate was produced not by engraving but by a special process of etching that remained obscure until it was reproduced in experiments by S. W. Hayter and Ruthven Todd in 1947. Rather than writing the text backwards directly on the plate, Blake wrote it out normally with 'a solution of asphaltum and resin in benzene upon a sheet of paper previously coated with a mixture of gum arabic and soap', after which this sheet was placed on a hot copper plate, pressed on it, and then soaked off. This left the text in reverse on the plate in acid resistant varnish. He then added the designs to the plate with a brush using the same sort of varnish solution, and the whole plate was etched with nitric acid, leaving text and design in relief. It was then inked by pressing ink on it from another plate or other flat surface and run through the press, producing an etched print, which was finally hand coloured in water-colour.[1] In his etched Prospectus addressed 'To the Public' in 1793, he was as private publisher advertising works in a style 'more ornamental, uniform, and grand, than any before discovered . . . at less than one fourth the expense'. Among them *America: A Prophecy* was offered for 10s. 6d.; *Visions of the Daughters of Albion* for 7s. 6d., as was *The*

Marriage of Heaven and Hell; and *Songs of Innocence* and *Songs of Experience* for 5s. each.[2] They were indeed a bargain.

His first works in this medium, not listed in the Prospectus, are the three tiny tractates, *There Is No Natural Religion* I and II and *All Religions Are One*, produced in 1788. These unusual works furnish a good introduction to some key concepts in Blake's thought because they set them forth explicitly in aphoristic form. We see here the beginnings of a sort of system of ideas.

Some readers are rather put off by the suggestion that Blake has 'system' or a 'philosophy'. He was not by any means a philosopher in any technical sense, nor was he ambitious to be one. But he was utterly convinced—to use philosophical language as shorthand for the moment—that the metaphysical assumptions that were dominant in his time, and had in fact been dominant since the Fall, yielded a false view of man, of God, and of being; and they produced religious, social, political, and intellectual institutions that kept man from realizing his potential for joy and wisdom—from realizing the divinity within him. These metaphysical assumptions, though they might appear in various contexts and forms, nevertheless constituted a sort of system, having a general coherence if looked at in the large perspective of the visionary prophet. And Blake, accordingly, felt the need to counteract them. But one cannot effectively attack a philosophical system within the limits of that system, accepting its rules and principles. So Blake needed a countersystem in order to expose error by means of it so that error could be cast out. Los, much later, in *Jerusalem*, might be thought of as speaking for Blake when he says: 'I must Create a System, or be enslav'd by another Mans / I will not Reason & Compare: my business is to Create'.[3]

The countersystem that Blake created is the coherent body of symbols that is organized by his myth of the Fall and regeneration of man with all its details. But within that encyclopaedic order are certain elements that can be treated as principles in a form that is amenable to dialectic. Though they do not constitute a body of principles that hangs together with tight logical rigour, they do have enough consistency to make it helpful to keep them in mind as one reads the poems and studies the art. In fact, Blake states many of these principles of his countersystem quite explicitly in a number of places.

The favourite targets of his countersystem are Bacon, Newton, and Locke, who become, as it were, the three heads of the philosophical Cerberus guarding the gates that keep man's mind in his version of hell, which he calls 'Ulro'. He might have chosen some others, for instance Hobbes, who was a greater enemy of imagination. But Bacon, Newton, and Locke symbolized for him the metaphysical assumptions of materialism and the exaltation of reason which generated a concept of man, of God, and of being, within which the social, religious, and political institutions kept man from realizing his divine potential. These thinkers did not invent the assumptions, but they did crystallize them in persuasive systems that Blake thought left no room for anything but a material reality, and no room for knowledge not deriving exclusively from rational ordering of the data of the five physical senses. Philosophically, Blake was an uncompromising idealist, and reality was for him not only mental, or ideal, but imaginative. The distinctive characteristic of man that made him human—and indeed connected him with God—was his imagination. A philosophical system that denied man his imagination not only denied man his being but also denied God.

His first statement of philosophical principles in the little tractates are directed most specifically at Bacon, perhaps in their form as well as in their content. They may be a parody of Bacon's 'Aphorisms on Man' in the *Magna Instauratio*. Peter Shaw, M.D., in his 1733 translation of Bacon's *Philosophical Works*, describes Bacon's aphoristic method:

In this aphoristical Manner, the Author proceeds thro' the Whole of the following Piece; which is no more than a continued String of Aphorisms; or summary Expressions of pure Matter of Science, in simple Language, without foreign Ornament; and upon the footing of competent Experience and Observation. . . . And as Aphorisms thus approach to Axioms; we should not despair of raising an Axiomatical Philosophy upon the Strength of the following Sett.[4]

Blake's tractates likewise are a 'string of aphorisms' which approach axioms, stated with a certitude coming from competent experience and observation. He could have patterned his aphorisms as most commentators suggest, after John Casper Lavater's *Aphorisms on Man*, which he liked and annotated. But it seems to me that Bacon's furnished him with a model that he could subject to his favourite method of attacking philosophical enemies, hoisting them with their own petards by parody or the exposure of self-contradictions.

Again, some of his aphorisms seem a very direct answer to Bacon. Bacon, for instance, writes in his first aphorism:

As man is but the Servant and Interpreter of Nature, he can work and understand no farther, than he shall, either in Action or Contemplation, observe of the Proceedings of Nature; to whose Laws he remains subject.[5]

And in his second aphorism Bacon puts limits on man's perception:

The Limits, therefore, of the human Power and Knowledge, lie in the Qualifications wherewith Man is by Nature endow'd for acting and perceiving; and again in the State of Things presented to him: and beyond these Limits his Instruments and Abilities can never reach.[6]

Blake's aphorisms speak quite directly to these points:

I. Mans perceptions are not bounded by organs of perception. he perceives more than sense (tho' ever so acute) can discover.

VII. The desire of Man being Infinite the possession is Infinite & himself Infinite.

Bacon goes on to predict that when a new organon is developed 'Man's Qualifications and Endowments' though limited, will be 'capable of bringing such Things before Judgment, and into Practice, as lie extremely remote from the ordinary Sense and Action; and again of conquering greater Difficulties in Works and Obscurities in Science, than any one at present knows so much as to wish for'. And Blake agrees that knowledge can be expanded: 'II. Reason or the ratio of all we have already known. is not the same that it shall be when we know more.' But his organon is to be the expanded imagination.

The 'Argument' of the third of the tractates, *All Religions Are One*, hints that, though the tractates as a group are directed at deism, to show that natural religion is impossible and that all religions derive from the imagination, he has Bacon also in mind: 'As the true method of knowing is experiment the true faculty of knowing must be the faculty which experiences.' Elsewhere he had noted the importance of experiment to Bacon: 'The Great Bacon he is Calld I call him the Little Bacon says that Every Thing must be done by Experiment.'[7]

Bacon in the *Magna Instauratio* was initiating, as the title implies, a huge scheme for new knowledge. Blake, in engraving his aphorisms on tiny plates, may have been mocking the pretentiousness of the 'little Bacon['s]' scheme, proposing his own instauration in miniature.

Blake organizes his string of aphorisms into three groups. The first one is a negative or critical group saying that naturally, which is to say physically, man is limited and that within the limits of natural man even 'the Philosophic & Experimental' would be at a standstill without 'the Poetic or Prophetic character', in other words, the imagination. The second string of aphorisms puts the matter positively, saying that man is not limited as the empiricists and materialists say he is, and ends with an 'Application': 'He who sees the Infinite in all things sees God. He who sees the Ratio only sees himself only. Therefore God becomes as we are, that we may be as he is.'

A few remarks on Blake's conception of perception and the imagination might be useful before commenting on the third set of aphorisms. When he says, in the second set, that 'Mans perceptions are not bounded by the organs of perception. he perceives more than sense (tho' ever so acute) can discover', and 'Reason or the ratio of all we have already known. is not the same that it shall be when we know more', Blake is joining issue with the empiricists on their own principle that knowledge is derived from perception; but his conception of perception is a very different one, as we shall see in a moment, for it is based on the idea that man and god have the imagination as a common and essential characteristic.

His conception of the imagination is a truly radical and comprehensive one, and it is central not only to his art and poetry but to his philosophy and religion. The imagination for him was the distinctive human characteristic, but it also is a divine characteristic. To put it rather simply, god is for Blake a cosmic imagination, not a separate 'other' from man—a vengeful sky-god issuing laws and concerned with material creation and cloaked in mystery—but a being possessing totally that vital and creative imagination which is man's essential life if he could but know it. Man and god are therefore of one substance, as it were, and for Blake the terms humanity and divinity are practically interchangeable. If man were to liberate his imagination from the clouds which obscure it, he would not only know god but would realize his own divinity. In 'The Everlasting Gospel', written much later, Blake says, 'Thou art a Man God is no more / Thy own humanity learn to adore'.[8] This may be heterodox, but it is fundamental.

Since man and God have imagination as a common ground of being, it becomes a matter of transcendent importance to get rid of the obstacles to the free exercise of the imagination, like philosophical ideas which restrict knowing to material existence, to what can be perceived by the five senses or inferred from data of those senses. Accordingly, Blake, in countering the prevalent philosophy of his time, takes as a fundamental concept of his countersystem a kind of perception that is not limited. He believes that any act of perception requires some imaginative synthesis of discrete sense data—which is why, in the first set of aphorisms, 'the Philosophic & Experimental' would be at a standstill without the 'Poetic or Prophetic character'. And, since this is so, imagination becomes an essential part of perception, if perception is going to lead to knowledge. Here he makes a large leap, based on his idealistic conception of being: if some imagination is essential to any kind of meaningful perception, then the more imagination that goes into perception, the better, and visions yield an enormous amount of knowledge.[9] A famous statement in his commentary on his painting of *The Last Judgment* illustrates: 'What it will be Questiond When the Sun rises do you not see a round Disk of fire somewhat like a Guinea O no no I see an Innumerable company of the Heavenly host crying Holy Holy Holy is the Lord God Almighty I question not my Corporeal or Vegetative Eye any more than I would Question a Window concerning a Sight I look thro it & not with it.'[10]

But spiritual perception, as he calls it, is not an escape into fantasy away from ordinary reality. It is, rather, a mode of perception which at its highest level reveals the nature of being and will alter other kinds of perception because it shows things in a new perspective. One would not always see the sun as a Hallelujah chorus, but if one looked at the sun with the idea in mind that it could be perceived as a praise of God, even seeing it as a ball of fire would be a different experience—it would be a *disc* only in a perception completely devoid of imaginative synthesis. Blake systematized his imaginative perception into four different levels, and perception could operate at any of them, given 'flexible senses'. We shall return to this idea later in more detail, but it may be useful to note it briefly here. At the highest level is 'fourfold' perception, which is like the sight of the sun just mentioned. At this level, one perceives with the most imagination, and the whole of being is revealed in symbolic visionary form. It might be called 'anagogic' vision, and the total form that being assumes for Blake at this level is that of Jesus, the 'one man' of whom we are all members. The existence of this level of perception should modulate the others. To go to the other end of the scale, single vision is mere physical perception. Twofold vision is like metaphoric perception, in which parts of being are seen as being connected with other parts. Threefold vision is a sort of transitional stage between twofold and fourfold, in which the mental orientation of the perceiver is altered and he begins to feel something of the joy in existence which the total vision at the fourfold level will finally reveal fully.

The objective of this theory of vision is not to justify an escape from 'reality' but to expand consciousness in a way that makes all seeing have meaning under the aspect of a divine reality and to recognize that the material world is in itself devoid of meaning but that, under the aspect of eternity, it can be seen that 'every thing that lives is Holy'.[11] Though Blake repeatedly denies even the existence of external material reality, he really wants to redeem it by assimilating it to a view of being in which it is no longer the only reality that it is in materialistic philosophies, but is only one aspect of a more comprehensive existence. If this could be done, the apocalypse, 'The Last Judgment', which Blake defines as 'an Overwhelming of Bad Art & Science',[12] will have occurred.

To go back now to the third string of aphorisms, *All Religions Are One*, Blake brings his ideas of perception as stated in the first two sets to bear on religion; and, on the basis of the unexpressed assumption that man and god have the imagination in common, says essentially that the world's religions all began with a perception of the imaginative nature of god but went astray in adapting this perception to weak understandings: 'Thus all sects of Philosophy are from the Poetic Genius adapted to the weakness of every individual.' In arguing that all religions are ultimately one, in being derived from a proper imaginative perception through the poetic genius, he is calling for a casting off of the obstacles to his kind of knowledge of God.

This is a rather long way round to seeing what is being said in Blake's tiny tractates, but they imply much more than they say directly; and the doctrines contained in them are also contained in other works, if only by implication.

For all their brevity, the tractates are astonishing works. In trying to make explicit some of the assumptions underlying the aphorisms, I have found it useful to quote from later formulations, where the meaning is more fully expressed. I hope I have not made the aphorisms mean more than they do, and I do not think I have. The fuller analysis that they merit would, in fact, show that many of the basic ideas of Blake's countersystem against Bacon, Newton, and Locke and the philosophy they symbolize were well developed at this time. This should not be surprising, since in 1789 when the tractates were engraved Blake was over thirty. Nevertheless, his ideas do develop in the works to come; but some of them, like his belief in the divinity of the imagination, do not essentially change.

Artistic forms, however, in which his ideas find expression, do change; or, rather, he tried a number of different forms. One of these is the two sets of contrasting lyrics, *Songs of Innocence and of Experience*, which everyone, even those who have thought Blake mad and incoherent in his other works, regards as marvels of the lyric art. Fine as these lyrics are individually, they belong in a total work, and, while it is possible to enjoy them as separate poems, as one can enjoy individual songs from Schubert's *Die Winterreise*, they are conceived as part of a whole work that is not a mere collection of lyrics but two sets of lyrics which together illustrate an idea, as the full title clearly states: *Songs of Innocence and of Experience Shewing the Two Contrary States of the Human Soul.*

Blake's very special concepts of Innocence and Experience, though embodied in short lyrics which take their point of departure from the conventions of pastoral poetry and poetry about and for children, have a deep psychological validity. They also describe a pattern in the development of human consciousness that appears repeatedly in other Romantic poetry, notably in Wordsworth's 'Immortality Ode'. The relationship between Innocence and Experience is not merely one of contrast but involves a cycle or a spiral from a simple Innocence into and through Experience and then on to a different, complex Innocence which, without rejecting Experience, transcends it in imaginative vision.

Between the extremes of the simple and wise, transcendent Innocence, the children and animals represented in the poems range from being pure symbols, used in the schematic development of the concept, to children who are found in a very harshly real situation, as is the Chimney Sweeper of *Innocence*; the poems that are not about children have the same sort of range. It might be worth while before proceeding farther to consider briefly the schematic development of the cyclical concept.

When C. A. Tulk sent Coleridge the songs to read, Coleridge liked most of them but objected to the line in 'Infant Joy', 'Thou dost smile', because a 'Babe of two days old does not, cannot *smile*—and innocence and the very truth of Nature must go together. Infancy is too holy a thing to be ornamented.'[13] He might also have objected to the babe's talking. Blake was not in this poem, or other poems of *Innocence* like it, representing nature but the pure 'state' of Innocence that can be seen, symbolically, in infancy. He would agree with Coleridge that infancy is a holy thing, not because it is a natural marvel but, as he suggests later in 'The Mental Traveller', because it represents a sort of incarnation of spirit and nature that contains the possibility for spiritualizing human life that was exemplified in Jesus. Here, however, the babe is used to show the pure joy of presumably unlimited potential. The first kind of Innocence in this schematic formulation is rich with joy and potential. The child follows his impulses with an unbridled enthusiasm—made possible not only by his own inherent human potential but also by his ignorance of the world—and he seeks joy without much thought as to whether what he does is good or evil and without awareness of harsh realities. He sees a lamb with the kind of delight that is possible if one need not consider how the animal will dress into roasts and chops. And he is able to take the church beadles, in 'Holy Thursday', as 'wise guardians of the poor' at face value because he lacks the knowledge of the world that would lead him to suspect anything else.

This kind of Innocence is appropriate to the child, but it is incomplete. A person who went through life with the *naïveté* of this state would simply be unable to cope with the inevitable harshness that life would bring, like poor crops and illness, let alone man-made oppression and hurts. When the Innocence of early childhood gives way to limitation of potential, and to hurt, we enter into the contrary state of Experience. The pure symbolic contrast to 'Infant Joy' is found in 'Infant Sorrow' in *Experience*, where the babe is born in pain, is bound and overcome:

> My mother groand! my father wept.
> Into the dangerous world I leapt:
> Helpless, naked, piping loud;
> Like a fiend hid in a cloud.

understood prejudice very well. In another poem, thematically related to 'The Little Black Boy' because the children in it also have black skins, he portrays a situation in which children, in this case chimney sweeps, are literally changed from white to black by a society that allows small children to be used for climbing chimneys to sweep them, and then finds warrant in their resulting blackness for viewing them as somehow sub-human and so for being released from any moral obligation toward them. In this poem, 'The Chimney Sweeper' of *Innocence*, the little sweep, who was literally 'sold' by his father to a master sweep at the age of six or even less, lives in a world of unrelieved blackness, sweeping chimneys during the day and sleeping on soot at night. He has no mother to teach him hopeful apocalyptic doctrine. His situation leads, literally, only to a future with twisted limbs, damaged eyesight, and possibly 'chimney sweep's cancer' of the scrotum from the soot, eventually to end as a ward of the parish.[17] He is about as far into the state of Experience as one can go. But this is a song of Innocence, and even here, though with terrible irony that is intensified by the pathetic situation of a child dreaming of the sweeps being set free from their coffins and washing in the river and running in the sunshine, some glimpse of a state beyond that of Experience must occur. For Tom Dacre, the new little sweep, this takes the form of a dream in which an angel, who talks like a kind but stuffy adult, takes enough of an interest in him to admonish him to 'be a good boy'. This is not much of a basis to sustain any vision, but, in the terrible circumstances, it seems to be enough to save Tom's humanity from being destroyed altogether, and 'Tho' the morning was cold, Tom was happy & warm' as he worked. In this poem the perspective of Innocence is severely tested, for the situation portrayed is all too real, as contemporary records show. Chimney sweeping by children was not outlawed until 1875.

It is the Innocence that dwells with knowledge, or organized innocence, that is in the central conception of the *Songs* the contrary state to Experience and one of the two states of the human soul. The Innocence that can be seen in childhood is a partial and schematically prior symbol for it. Childhood expresses the joyful, instinctive quality essential to all Innocence, but it does not portray the complexity that is the distinguishing characteristic of the organized state. This is expressed not only in the complex *Songs of Innocence* like the poems just discussed but also in the synthesis of the two sets of songs as they come to be simultaneously present in the mind after one has read them.

Yet one cannot regard the simpler songs as merely expressing the simple level of Innocence. Reading both sets of songs involves us in a sort of spiralling development of context. We come to recognize that the two sets each imply the other, and on successive readings we bring even to such simple songs as 'Infant Joy', which can be seen as a symbolic stepping stone leading toward the idea of organized Innocence, some of the perspective that was gained from the other songs, with the result that it no longer seems quite so simple.

For this reason the several pairs of matching lyrics in the *Songs*, which at first seem merely to express two contrasting points of view, or two stages of life, must be taken to represent them schematically in a developing conception that is a synthesis of the two. The distinction between a song of Innocence and one of Experience is, in fact, sometimes hard to draw. 'The Chimney Sweeper' of *Innocence* is much more bitter than its counterpart in *Experience* and is a song of the first set only because of the faintly felt hope in Tom's dream. The first issue of *Songs of Innocence* included four songs that were in later issues transferred to *Songs of Experience*: 'The Little Girl Lost', 'The Little Girl Found', 'The Voice of the Bard', and 'The Schoolboy'.

The two most famous matching lyrics are 'The Lamb' and 'The Tyger', connected not only by the naturally contrasting character of the animals portrayed but by the questions in both poems asking who made them. 'The Lamb' is as gentle and serene as 'The Tyger' is terrifying and powerful. The etching of 'The Lamb' shows a naked boy talking to a lamb which nuzzles his hand as the other sheep rest or graze between a little brook and barn. The song builds up an association between the lamb and the child through a common relationship they have with Jesus (who 'calls himself a lamb' and 'became a little child') and ends, before the refrain:

> I a child & thou a lamb,
> We are called by his name.

Child and lamb are united in the Incarnation and in the Agnus Dei.

Rhythmically, the interior lines of 'The Lamb' that are framed by the refrain-like lines at the beginning and end of the stanza are the same as those of 'The Tyger'. But the framing lines make all the difference in the music of the song, whose metrical effects and repeated lines suggest very strongly that Blake probably had music in mind here. The last two syllables of the framing lines, 'made thee' in the first stanza and 'tell thee' and 'bless thee' in the second, were surely intended to occur on notes that were held for at least one full beat each. The lovely setting of this song by Vaughan Williams, with only the clean line of a solo oboe to capture the pastoral feeling, lends support to this. It is curious that Williams intensely disliked the poem, referring to it as that 'horrible little lamb', and at first refused to set it, but he awoke in the night with 'a tune for that beastly little lamb' and quite properly thought it 'rather a good tune'.[18]

The questions the child asks in 'The Lamb' have clear answers, supplied by the child, in the Christian context. The questions of which 'The Tyger' is entirely composed have no such answers. They are not an example of any kind of rhetorical question but very real questions asked by a speaker, whose identity is not at all clear, addressed to the tiger itself. Answers seem somehow irrelevant or inadequate. The real answers to the questions are embodied in the dread but awesomely fascinating image of the mighty beast itself that is evoked not so much by description of the tiger but of its creation, in two dozen short lines. Such description as we get in the images through which the tiger is evoked avoid the most distinctive features of the natural animal *felis Tigris*, except for possibly his eyes and the fearful symmetry of his stripes, and instead mention his heart, whose sinews were twisted by a transcendent shoulder, and his brain, forged in a cosmic furnace. The only thing clear about him is that he is a spiritual, imaginative form of a tiger, not one in a zoo.

And perhaps it is best simply to let it go at that and take E. M. Forster's advice not even to try to talk about him. This lyric in all its powerful ambiguity approaches absolute art in poetry and stubbornly resists critical attempts to explain its meaning. But critics, including this one, have not been entirely willing to let all questions about it remain unanswered, if only in an effort to understand a little better why it is so powerful. Almost inevitably, the practical questions asked about the image of the tiger have taken a moral form: Is the tiger 'good' or 'evil', or does his ambiguity arise from his being neither or some of both? There used to be more critical votes for 'evil' than now, or for a mixture in taking the poem as a 'probing of good and evil'. But with the development of modern Blake scholarship—'the Blake industry' it has been called—which has shown that Blake rejected the normative moral categories of good and evil, especially at the time the poem was written, those who take a negative view of the tiger regard him as 'Urizenic', the creation by the demiurge for the material world. Evidence for interpretations comes both from parallels in Blake's other works and from outside. Neither the text by itself nor the etched illustration, showing a tiger that is not fearful at all, is of much help.

There is little question about the tiger's awesomeness and cosmic power. But it is important, in the study of Blake's works as a whole, to try to determine, if we can, what are the components of that awesomeness and power—how we are to take him, and how he is related to the lamb with whom he is clearly connected in the text. There is also no question about his having a genuinely fearful aspect in his 'fearful symmetry'. But the question that must arise is what is the other side of the symmetry and does it also contribute to fearfulness, or is it symmetrically opposite to it? It seems to me that any answers to these questions which substantially diminish the essential ambiguity of the poem or seriously limit the fearfulness of the symmetry are on the wrong track, because they would explain away some of the force of the poem. But it also seems to me possible to view the symmetry as containing an essentially positive component without really hurting its ambiguity. Blake's drafts of the poem in his Notebook show, I think, that he started out with a powerful symbolic tiger but had strong negative feelings about it that appear most clearly in a cancelled stanza, which grammatically completed the question, 'What dread hand? & what dread feet?'

> Could fetch it [the heart] from the furnace deep
> And in the horrid ribs dare steep
> In the well of sanguine woe
> In what clay & in what mould
> Were thy eyes of fury rolld[?][19]

In the next draft he went to the other extreme, removing all the dread but retaining the fifth stanza, which is crucial to the poem and which parallel passages in his other work at the time suggest

1. Portrait of William Blake by John Linnell

The SICK ROSE

O Rose thou art sick.
The invisible worm.
That flies in the night
In the howling storm:

Has found out thy bed
Of crimson joy:
And his dark secret love
Does thy life destroy.

2. 'The Sick Rose' from *Songs of Experience*

as being in some way or other a description of a favourable outcome to the tiger's creation. (If these parallels do not settle the matter, they are awkward facts to be got over in any attempt to show that the fifth stanza is negative in tone.) Finally, in the poem as Blake etched it, both elements were brought together.

In the context of Innocence and Experience, the tiger is related to the lamb as its opposite, but the question is whether it is its 'contrary', which is to say a force of an opposite but harmonious kind, or its 'negation', a force which denies and would destroy the lamb. Both have been suggested by critics. It seems to me that it is the former. In the context of Innocence and Experience, the tiger can be seen as an image of cosmic wrath and energy that is needed to destroy some of the elements of Experience, though not the state itself, when they threaten the existence of the state symbolized by the lamb—or Lamb. All through the *Songs* Innocence has been associated with light, but gentle light. The light of the tiger is fiery as he burns in 'the forests of the night'.

To say this does not, I think, eliminate ambiguity. There are profound questions, as our own age knows very well, whenever a power like that symbolized by the tiger comes into being, even if its creation seems warranted. Is the cosmic wrath and energy that can be glimpsed in the dread tiger, and that seems to bring about some kind of destruction of the forces of oppression in the fifth stanza, something which will depart when no longer needed? Will the tiger turn gentle and weep 'ruby tears' like the lion in 'Little Girl Lost'?

The crux in any reading of 'The Tyger' is the fifth stanza:

> When the stars threw down their spears
> And water'd heaven with their tears:
> Did he smile his work to see?
> Did he who made the Lamb make thee?

This puts the question directly, asking whether the creator of the Lamb was also the creator of the tiger and if so was he pleased with his creation? It calls for a Yes or No answer, as the 'What' questions that make up the rest of the poem do not. The questions used to be translated into conventional religious terms as the ancient question, Could God create both good and evil? The question, 'Did he smile his work to see', it seems to me, makes such a translation not quite to the point. In any event, the answers that might

C

be suggested—and few commentators would go much farther than suggesting answers—depend largely on who the creator is. If the creator is not God but the demiurge, as Miss Kathleen Raine suggests, approaching the poem through possible sources in Jacob Boehme and the Hermetica and glossing it from parallel imagery in Urizen's account of his fall in *The Four Zoas*, the answer to the first question would be No but the answer to the second would be Yes, followed by remorse. But Miss Raine is a subtle reader of the poem, and, while it is for her 'the presentation of the problem of evil as he [Blake] found it in the Hermetic and Gnostic tradition' she feels that the questions remain unanswered because the answer would be 'a no or yes of such depth and complexity', and no because Blake had no answer.[20]

A mere Yes or No would leave the issue unsettled, and I would agree that the questions remain essentially unanswered, but for different reasons. If 'The Tyger' is considered in the context of Blake's work alone, it seems to me that he could be regarded as a providential creation *for*—not of or by—the fallen world of Experience. If we take the stars in this crucial stanza as having a meaning near to that which they had in works closely contemporary with the poem, as symbolizing oppression, and also take their throwing down their spears in this context as indicating some kind of defeat, then the answers to both questions are probably Yes—but a Yes of such deep ambivalence in the context of the genuine fearfulness of the beast as to leave the questions without definitive answers.

It seems almost certain that Blake sang 'The Lamb'. 'The Tyger' may be another matter. No musical setting that I know of does it justice. It seems a text to be chanted rather than sung. Henry Crabb Robinson gave an impressive rendering of it which Lamb heard, but Robinson apparently did not sing it, nor did he include notice of his having heard Blake do so.[21]

Others of the songs, especially the pastoral songs of *Innocence*, probably were sung by Blake. And it seems to me that they are metrically clarified if a possible musical rhythm is taken into account. Musically, 'Spring', for instance, fits very nicely to part of the rhythm of the theme of J. S. Bach's bourée in the C major unaccompanied 'cello suite, No. 3, and the music points up the fact that the rhythmical phrase in this poem extends over the whole stanza, suggesting that it should not be read with marked pauses

the ends of the lines. The tempo probably should also be a bit
quicker than that at which one would normally read it aloud, with
the syllables of the single word 'merrily' in the next to the last line
of the stanza being stretched out. The first stanza reads:

> Sound the Flute!
> Now it's mute.
> Birds delight
> Day and Night.
> Nightengale
> In the dale
> Lark in Sky
> Merrily
> Merrily Merrily to welcome in the Year.

And Bach's bourrée begins:

I think there is in the etched design a suggestion of the combination
of the shorter rhythmic pattern of the individual lines with the
longer rhythms of the musical phrase in the stanza. On the left-
hand side of the plate the decorative tendrils curve tightly, and on
the right side they are looser, following the pattern of the stanza.
Visual rhythms reinforce aural ones.

Songs of Innocence and of Experience, which I have been able
merely to touch on here, are marvels from any point of view. They
are certainly marvels of poetic concentration; and, before leaving
them, I should like to note, if only briefly, a poem which readily
shows some of Blake's ability to absorb a natural object in what
George Whalley calls a 'poetic event' and make the meaning
explode with symbolic resonance.[22] 'The Sick Rose' is a tiny poem
of eight lines, consisting of a brief opening sentence and only one
other sentence:

> O Rose thou art sick.
> The invisible worm,
> That flies in the night
> In the howling storm:

Has found out thy bed
Of crimson joy:
And his dark secret love
Does thy life destroy.

The rose is seen in 'twofold' metaphoric vision immediately at th
word 'sick', a word more applicable to humans than to rose
producing a submerged metaphor of personification. Then th
worm, which in nature might be connected with the rose, is als
altered by being made trebly unseen and secret in not only bein
invisible but flying in the night and in a storm. Finally, the flowe
bed is transformed into a 'bed of crimson joy', connoting the joyf
sexuality of innocence. The meaning is suddenly expanded b
putting this kind of love in opposition to the worm's 'dark secr
love', which destroys the life of the rose. Thematically, the ros
the worm, and the flowerbed—the natural elements Blake star
with—undergo a visionary expansion of meaning in which th
natural elements, by metaphorical transformation, are seen
participating in a drama involving two kinds of love and the worl
views they imply. Natural elements, by an altered word or tw
become a focus of metaphysical relationships. It is hard to conceiv
of much greater or more efficient poetic concentration than this.

The etched illustration shows a female figure in distress stretchin
partly out of a spherical form that suggests a rosebud into which
worm seems to be entering. A bush with thorns and the leaves
a rose bend down, and on its branches are a caterpillar and tw
other female figures in attitudes of grief.

In taking *Songs of Innocence* and *Songs of Experience* together,
have violated chronology, because the first was etched in 1789 an
the latter not until 1794; but of course they belong together. T
return to 1789, we find Blake producing his first etched 'propheti
book', the lovely *Book of Thel*. Thel is a character who wants t
remain at the first level of Innocence, shunning the state of Ex
perience, which would at once fulfill her but also involve her wit
the pain of the world or 'generation', which she could transcend
as she is told by the voice from her own grave which she visits
But she elects not to commit herself to the full cycle of human lif
and pulls back, to remain unfulfilled and a virgin, to fade awa
without a human identity as anything. All the beings that The
talks with, the golden cloud that floats down to her, the lily wh
has a function in feeding the lamb, and the earth as clod of clay

ave a function in the cycle of Innocence-Experience-wise In-
ocence; but Thel does not. This work is completely accessible to
nyone who wants to be able to say he has penetrated the Blakean
ngle far enough to have read at least one of the 'prophetic books',
o which we now turn.

4 | The Marriage of Heaven and Hell

During the time Blake was producing *Songs of Experience*, he wa also writing and etching a work of a very different kind, *Th Marriage of Heaven and Hell*, begun, as indicated in a chronologica reference in the text, in 1790 but not completed until 1792 or 179 It is a strange work, a kind of philosophical manifesto, partly i satiric form, affirming the polar nature of being and the need f a change in man's perception so that this polar nature can b recognized. The immediate object of the work, arising from i satiric theme, was to expose and reject the normative moral cate gories of Good and Evil of orthodox religion by showing tha Good and Evil are merely abstractions, distortions of the vita 'contraries' that inform all being and that must be allowed t function without restraint in human life. Good and Evil as ordinaril conceived deny each other and are hence what Blake later cal 'negations'. In *The Marriage*, he explains 'what the religious ca Good & Evil' really are: 'Good is the passive that obeys Reason [Evil is the active springing from Energy. Good is Heaven. Evil Hell.'[1] And he 'marries' them—or rather reunites them—as reaso and energy in this philosophical manifesto. But for satirical purpose he retains the orthodox terms through much of the work an seems to be turning ordinary morality upside down as he exalt energy as Hell. Some readers, including Swinburne, have accord ingly misunderstood his purpose and have taken him to be satanist.[2]

The Marriage is the second statement in his philosophical counter system, the tractates being the first. *Songs of Innocence and of Ex perience* could also be included as part of this in the sense that tw sets of songs develop a concept in moral philosophy also involvin a kind of contrariety, which, however, is somewhat different fron

hat in *The Marriage*. Blake's manifesto in *The Marriage* is, as I
uggested the tractates were, satiric in form. It seems appropriate
or a countersystem to be partly satiric, making error clearer by
xposing it as ridiculous. The immediate object of satire in *The
Marriage* is Emmanuel Swedenborg, though the whole rationalist
eligious complex of which Swedenborg is a part is the real target.

As was mentioned earlier, Blake and Catherine had for a brief
ime become officially Swedenborgians, even signing a set of
esolutions at a conference of the New Church in London in 1789.
But Blake quickly became disillusioned and was sharply critical of
Swedenborg's apparent extrapolation of earthly predestinarianism
nto the next world in a way that would seem to turn heaven partly
t least into a replica of earth—and would certainly seem to deny
he possibility of the apocalypse which Blake worked to bring
bout, through art, all his life. Blake was probably attracted to
Swedenborg because Swedenborg, a scientist, had experienced
visions and had based a religion on them. But as he went farther
nto Swedenborg's works, after finding much to admire in those
of 1784 and 1788, he came to feel that the scientist turned visionary
was, after all, one of the religious reasoners: that his conversion to
vision was incomplete and his visions contaminated. Later on he
was more charitable toward Swedenborg, calling him a 'Samson
horn by the Churches', or a 'divine teacher' who has 'done much
good, and will do much good'. But even then he seldom failed to
add that Swedenborg was nevertheless 'wrong in endeavouring to
explain to the *rational* faculty what the reason cannot comprehend'.[3]
In *The Marriage* he showed little charity. Where Swedenborg had
described in elaborate detail in his *Heaven and Hell* (1784) how the
'hells', of which there were not one but many, were kept separate
from heaven and ruled by angels, Blake marries them. And where
Swedenborg has said 'Without equilibrium there is neither action
nor reaction', Blake, rejecting equilibrium as dead, static, explicitly
opposes to it the main principle of *The Marriage*: 'Without Contraries is no progression. Attraction and Repulsion, Reason and
Energy, Love and Hate, are necessary to Human existence.'[4]
Formally, *The Marriage* proceeds by alternating sections of theoretical exposition and 'memorable fancies'. The latter are parodies
of Swedenborg's 'memorable relations' among the angels, the
accounts, written in very matter-of-fact language, of angelic
conversations.

Swedenborg is not mentioned in the poetic account given in a letter that Blake wrote Flaxman in 1800, speaking of his 'lot in Heaven' and of the spiritual events that were important in it. That part of the poem is worth quoting fully because it contains element important to the background of *The Marriage* to which I shall have occasion to refer later. After expressing gratitude to Flaxman for his friends in his 'lot on Earth', Blake tells of his lot in heaven:

> Now my lot in the Heavens is this, Milton lov'd
> me in childhood & shew'd me his face.
> Ezra came with Isaiah the Prophet, but Shakespeare
> in riper years gave me his hand;
> Paracelsus & Behmen appear'd to me, terrors
> appear'd in the Heavens above
> And in Hell beneath, & a mighty & awful change
> threatened the Earth.
> The American war began. All its dark horrors
> passed before my face
> Across the Atlantic to France. Then the French
> Revolution commenc'd in thick clouds,
> And My Angels have told me that seeing such
> visions I could not subsist on the Earth,
> But by my conjunction with Flaxman, who knows to
> forgive Nervous Fear.[5]

Blake was in Felpham at this time, grateful to Flaxman for his 'present Happiness' in his cottage, building a new life under the patronage of William Hayley, painting miniatures and doing other work that he hoped would provide more earthly happiness than he had enjoyed. For the moment, he seemed a prophet of apocalyptic revolution gone underground out of a 'nervous fear' that was to be justified in the trial for treason at the end of the Felpham sojourn. But this came later. A decade earlier, in *The Marriage* and in his prophetic accounts of the revolutions in France and America he was more forthright, responding to visions of heaven and hell that were more powerful than those to be found in Swedenborg's memorable relations among the angels. And he was formulating metaphysical conceptions to match, in which Swedenborg was of little help.

Among the men to appear to him, as noted in the poem, were Paracelsus (Theophrastus Bombastus von Hohenheim, the German physician and alchemist) and 'Behmen' (Jacob Boehme, the 'Teutonic Theosophist' popularized in England by William Law). In *The Marriage* Blake explicitly devalues Swedenborg in comparison with these men, by a factor of ten thousand to one: 'Any man of mechanical talents may from the writings of Paracelsus or Jacob Behmen, produce ten thousand volumes of equal value with Swedenborg's.' It is rather hard to find any very direct influences on Blake from Paracelsus—and tracing influences in Blake is a most uncertain business at best because everything he borrows becomes very much his own. But there do seem to be some echoes of Boehme in Blake's development of his idea of the contraries. Some of the vigour of his rejection of Swedenborg may have come about because Swedenborg's religious ideas seemed to him so thin compared with those of Boehme.

But Blake hardly needed Boehme as a source for his idea of the contraries. Heraclitus' idea that being comes from strife or subsists in strife was a commonplace that appeared everywhere, in a variety of places in poetry ranging from Spenser to Pope. The Pythagoreans founded a whole system of the universe on polarities; and Bayle's dictionary made available extended accounts of polar metaphysics in discussing Manicheanism.[6] Even the great—or, as Blake would have it, 'the little'—Bacon took basic oppositions into account as aspects of nature, calling them 'Transcendentals or Adventitious Conditions of Essences' (*De Dignitate*). Blake had only to adapt to his own purposes ideas that were readily available.

Moreover, since he was in *The Marriage* interested in reunifying human life, which he saw as being split by rationalized religion, into normative moral categories of Good and Evil and since his imagination was a visionary one that had to develop a total order of imagery in mythic form, he was perfectly capable of re-inventing this idea himself. Polarities, opposites, dualisms are simply fundamental experiences in human life and nature—in sexuality, in bilateral bodies, in root ideas like hot and cold, and so on—and mythic thinking deeply reflects these. So, in their own way, do the ordinary concepts of Good and Evil. But to Blake, dividing existence into Good and Evil implied a religion based on abstract reason rather than a direct relationship with God, a morality of negative commandments which could be utilized to suppress the impulse to know God, and it could generate or at least support institutions like monarchies. The typical manifestation in man's life in the world was 'corporeal war', in which one part of the human race tried to destroy another part. Good and Evil were religio-moral ideas which in political action led inevitably to oppression and destruction. And in religion they implied a god to match, whom Blake early called 'Nobo-daddy' (i.e., nobody's father) and later identified as Urizen (from, possibly, material existence: 'your-eyes-on', from 'horizon', or from '*your*-reason,' which is to say, not mine).

Later on he would make allowance for evil, of a kind, as having a real existence. But in *The Marriage* he wanted, as did his disciple Yeats, to get beyond good and evil. He wanted not only to redeem the contraries from their distorted state as Good and Evil in material-istic, rationalized religion but also to show the way to a knowledge of the real ground in which the contraries in human life would be seen as creative rather than destructive; and that ground was the imagination which connected man with God.

Pope invokes the strife of opposites in *The Essay on Man* as inevitable though not perhaps desirable:

> Better for Us, perhaps, it might appear,
> Were there all harmony, all virtue here;
> That never air or ocean felt the wind;
> That never passion discomposed the mind.
> But All subsists by elemental strife;
> And Passions are the elements of Life.
> The gen'ral Order, since the whole began,
> Is kept in Nature, and is kept in Man.
>
> (I, 165–72)

The ground in which opposites operate and are harmonized is nature or man himself. And the opposites are merely accepted as necessary but uncomfortable facts of life. Pope's harmony is more an equilibrium than a harmony. In his idea of the contraries, as we have seen, Blake is not satisfied with equilibrium. His contraries interact with vigour. But more important, his contraries are not harmonized in some external order; 'the gen'ral Order' is not 'kept' by anything, certainly not in nature or fallen man who believes in the efficacy of nature as providing a cosmic order. For Blake the 'order' is the interaction of the contraries in the cosmic imagination of which man is a part. 'Reason and Energy' in *The Marriage*—which might be roughly equated with contraction, or form, and expansion, or genius—are essential to human life in

Blake's special sense of the word 'human'—a state in which man's imagination has been liberated from the 'mind-forg'd manacles' of false philosophies (of the kind which Pope subscribes to) and man has realized the essential divinity of his own nature. In this state, the contraries, though opposed to each other, are not negations bent on each other's destruction and hence do not need to be harmonized by some external agency. If, for purposes of conceptual discrimination, we say that they function in some kind of unifying 'field' which could perhaps be thought of as a universe in which they coexist in their creative conflict, that field is the totality of being in the cosmic imagination.

Negations like Good and Evil attempt to hinder and even destroy. Blake's contraries do not. They pull in different directions, vigorously so in the 'mental war' which at the apocalypse will replace corporeal; but they work, as it were, with mutual respect and love. They have an inherent unity in being what they are, and the identity of each implies the existence of the other, somewhat as male implies female, and vice versa. Unity for Blake 'is as much in a Part as in the Whole' in art and in everything else.[7]

Since, moreover, all of being is organized as contraries, Blake's contraries do not disappear in some sort of higher synthesis. Nor is the 'progression' in which they function one in which they change their identities, as the opposites do in Hegelian dialectic. The progression in human life to which they are essential is the progression of continued creativity; and if it goes anywhere it goes toward fuller realization of the divinity that is in humanity through continued fruits of a life lived with the divine imagination, rather than nature, as the ground of being.

Blake's doctrine of the contraries is quite clearly not merely Heraclitean or anything else. It is his own. To be sure, Heraclitus, like Blake, criticized a spokesman of the religious establishment of his time, Homer, for not allowing room for the contraries in his scheme of being.[8] Blake's objective is to put forth an idea which, if taken seriously, would help bring about the apocalypse, a gigantic change of man's mind which would show that 'mental things are alone real' and that real freedom in its most comprehensive sense was not only possible but necessary. *The Marriage* is an apocalyptic document. One of its tasks was to expound the doctrine of contraries, which we have just been considering. The other was to show by what means the real nature of being could be known: in other words, to use philosophical jargon, what kind of epistemology was necessary to know real existence. I touched earlier on his expanded sense-perception which included the potential for synoptic fourfold vision and other lesser degrees of vision. This expanded sense-perception, which involves as much imagination as possible, now becomes another main theme in *The Marriage*, taking up most of its middle section.

I have dwelt this long on the main ideas of *The Marriage* partly because they are important for later works but also partly to avoid long digressions in the discussion of the work itself, which is a fascinating mixture of satire, apocalyptic doctrine, philosophical doctrine, and, as Northrop Frye has remarked, 'rowdy guffaws'.[9]

The Marriage, comprising twenty-seven plates, is arranged structurally into an opening Argument and then into six alternating expository sections each followed by a 'memorable fancy'. Added to it is a 'Song of Liberty' that applies politically the ideas developed in *The Marriage*. Thematically considered, the work divides into three main sections, the first dealing with the idea of contraries (to plate 6), the second with expanded sense-perception (from plate 6 through 14), and a third returning to the contraries again in the light of thematic development of the idea of sense-perception (plate 15 through 24).

The title-page shows a number of embracing figures flying upward from an abyss bounded on the left by the fires of 'Hell' and on the right by the clouds of 'Heaven' through a nether sky to a walk among trees. And the Argument suggests that some kind of change is imminent in its opening lines,

> Rintrah roars & shakes his fires in the burdend air;
> Hungry clouds swag on the deep [.]

Blake could not expect his reader to know who Rintrah is, for this character makes his first appearance here. But the revolutionary mood is clear enough—and, as Erdman suggests, Rintrah may be an ironic version of Pitt, and the fires and clouds of the opening lines were appearing in France.[10] The Argument proper gives an account of what happened to the 'just man' in a little fable:

> Once meek, and in a perilous path,
> The just man kept his course along
> The vale of death.

Roses are planted where thorns grow.
And on the barren heath
Sing the honey bees.

But then the perilous path itself was domesticated, 'planted', and Adam, the natural man was created: 'on the bleached bones / Red clay brought forth', Adam's name literally meaning red clay. The Fall has occurred in the entrenchment of material creation, and the path of the just man (which in Proverbs iv, 18 'is as the shining light' though here it was 'perilous' to those who do not understand the contraries in human life) has been usurped by the 'villain', and humility has been left to the serpent while the just man 'rages in the wilds'. The repetition of the opening lines at the end of the argument suggests that this situation will soon change. Rintrah may express God's anger in Isaiah xxxiv and hint at the change that follows it in Isaiah xxxv. Blake gives the scriptural references in the next section of *The Marriage*.

The first expository section, on plate 3, states the theme of the contraries already referred to and also introduces the satire on Swedenborg and the new heaven of his New Church. 'Heaven' is here, as it usually is in Blake, ironic. Swedenborg's new heaven was begun thirty-three years before, a time period which makes its beginning identical with Blake's own birth and also suggests that, since Christ was thirty-three at the crucifixion and resurrection, the new heaven was brought about by his death. This is reinforced by Swedenborg's being 'the Angel sitting at the tomb; his writings are the linen clothes folded up'. Swedenborg's theology has only to do with the dead Christ worshipped by material religion. But as 'new heaven is begun . . . the Eternal Hell revives', being revived not only through the negations of Good and Evil necessary to a religion postulating a heaven of smug righteousness but also revived in the ironic sense in which Blake uses 'Hell' in *The Marriage* —the repressed energy that is excluded from the realm of being by conceptions such as heaven, whether new or old. Then Blake states the main theme of this section:

Without Contraries is no progression. Attraction and Repulsion, Reason and Energy, Love and Hate, are necessary to Human existence. From these contraries spring what the religious call Good & Evil. Good is the passive that obeys Reason [.] Evil is the active springing from Energy. Good is Heaven. Evil is Hell.

The next section, 'The Voice of the Devil', is not called a 'memorable fancy', but it works like one, introducing a concrete dramatic element to follow the dogmatic opening section. The devil's statements have often been taken as those of Blake himself. To be sure, Blake, as one of the active contraries among mankind, would certainly incline to be 'of the devil's party', as he said Milton was. And we would not go too far astray to let the devil speak for Blake —not as Satan but as what 'the religious' think of the devil as being. But as a partisan spokesman for energy, the devil is not much interested in the marriage of reason and energy. Accordingly, when as a contradiction to one of the errors that 'All bibles or sacred codes' have been guilty of, he asserts that 'Man has no Body distinct from his Soul for that calld Body is a portion of the Soul discernd by the five Senses, the chief inlets of Soul in this age', the devil is speaking the truth—but not quite the whole truth: he avoids mention of the interaction of body and soul required by Blake's theory. Likewise, when he says 'Energy is the only life and is from the Body [admitting, perhaps, that he should have acknowledged body in the previous statement] and Reason is the bound or outward circumference of Energy', he is again overstating.

The second expository section gives a penetrating psychological account of the authoritarian personality: 'Those who restrain desire, do so because theirs is weak enough to be restrained; and the restrainer or reason usurps its place & governs the unwilling.' And he goes on to apply it to the growth of authoritarian religion, saying that a long institutionalized system of repression all but destroys desire altogether. Even Milton was not free of restraint when writing of 'Angels and God', but he could write 'at liberty when of Devils & Hell, . . . because he was a true Poet and of the Devils party without knowing it'.

Blake is quoted from the next section more often than from any other place, for we now move to a view of Hell, where we first see a mighty devil etching a pair of lines drawn from Chatterton on the side of the cliff:

> How do you know but ev'ry Bird that cuts the airy way,
> Is an immense world of delight, clos'd by your senses five?

This applies the idea from the first tractate of *There Is No Natural Religion* that 'From a perception of only 3 senses or 3 elements none could deduce a fourth or fifth'. The narrator collects seventy

'Proverbs of Hell', thinking 'that as the sayings used in a nation, mark its character, so the Proverbs of Hell, show the nature of Infernal wisdom better than any description of buildings or garments'. These proverbs invite comparison with those in the Old Testament, and may be intended to form part of the 'Bible of Hell' announced at the end of *The Marriage*, developing some of the devil's codes as 'Proverbs' develops moral virtue. In general, the proverbs exalt the active over the passive ('Expect poison from the standing water') and also exalt excess ('The road of excess leads to the palace of wisdom') as opposed to restraint and moderation, which are adventitious limits. In counselling 'excess', therefore, the proverbs adopt the rhetoric and categories of 'the religious', for infernal wisdom sees everything as good, even the pride of the peacock, the lust of the goat, the wrath of the lion, and the nakedness of woman, all of which come from God. 'Prudence', says one of the funnier proverbs, 'is a rich ugly old maid courted by Incapacity' (no. 4). One of Blake's infernal proverbs has passed into pretty common usage: 'The tygers of wrath are wiser than the horses of instruction' (no. 44). If, as the proverb says, 'Exuberance is Beauty', the proverbs are beautiful indeed.

In the third expository section that follows, Blake takes up the theme of perception again, giving his adaptation of a fairly popular account of the rise of religions that appears in the work of Colin Maclaurin, the interpreter of Newton; Richard Payne Knight's *A Discourse on the Worship of Priapus* . . .; in Coleridge; and in Shelley.[11] In Blake's succinct version of the process, the 'ancient Poets animated all sensible objects with Gods or Geniuses' giving them the names and properties of nature, cities, and nations and of 'whatever their enlarged & numerous senses could perceive'; then a 'system was formed, which some took advantage of & enslav'd the vulgar' by abstracting the 'mental deities from their objects' and making them real and mysterious, thus creating 'Priesthood'; the next step was that they 'pronounced that the Gods had ordered such things'; thus, the account concludes, 'men forgot that All deities reside in the human breast'. What starts out as the imaginative exaltation of natural objects is abstracted from objects, made a mystery requiring priestly interpreters, and finally turned into laws. In his annotations to Reynolds' discourses, Blake objected to the same sort of thing in Reynolds' making a general pattern into a norm from which every deviation is a 'deformity'. Since Blake often rejected external nature as non-existent, the importance he attached to the objects of nature in this passage may seem inconsistent, but it really is not. He is wholly consistent in saying that perception cannot be considered apart from an object, or at least discrete percepts cannot. Doing so leads to chaos: 'Deduct from a rose its redness, from a lilly its whiteness from a diamond its hardness from a spunge its softness from an oak its heighth from a daisy its lowness & rectify every thing in Nature as the Philosophers do. & then we shall return to Chaos & God will be compelld to be Excentric if he Creates O happy Philosopher.' 'The substance,' he says, 'gives tincture to the accident & makes it physiognomic'.[12]

The 'memorable fancy' that follows parodies Swedenborg's blandly reported conversations with the angels. Blake has two of his favourite prophets, Ezekiel and Isaiah, in for dinner and asks them how they could be so sure that God spoke to them. Isaiah replied that he 'saw no God, nor heard any, in a finite organical perception' but saw the infinite in everything and was 'perswaded, & remain confirm'd; that the voice of honest indignation is the voice of God', and so wrote. Ezekiel gives an account of the poetic genius as the source of all perception. After dinner the narrator asks about lost works of both, but learns there are none; he also inquires about their extreme behaviour, and is told that they had to behave that way and not care for the consequences. Ezekiel said he went barefoot for three years for the same reason as 'our friend Diogenes the Grecian'. In *The Island in the Moon*, Blake, it will be recalled, cast himself as Quid the Cynic, a modern Diogenes.

Plate 14, illustrated by a cadaverous recumbent body over which hovers a vigorous figure coming out of fire, brings the section on sense-perception to a climax, in the prophecy announced here that the apocalypse is at hand. The narrator exuberantly commands the 'covering cherub' guarding the tree of life to leave, and 'when he does, the whole creation will be consumed, and appear infinite. and holy whereas it now appears finite & corrupt'. This will come about by the 'improvement of sensual enjoyment' and the cleansing of perception, and these will be possible when the narrator—and here the *persona* clearly becomes Blake—has expunged the Cartesian notion that the body is distinct from the soul, which he will do by 'printing in the infernal method', by the 'corrosives' of philosophical criticism and satire in the etched form of his illuminated books.

The previous plate with its prophecy and reference to printing leads to the remarkable 'memorable fancy' of the printing house in hell, which is Blake's version of the allegory of the cave. This is a rich section not easily summarized, but in general it develops both the idea of expanded sense-perception and the contraries together, in moving through five chambers into a sixth. In the first, sensual enjoyment and perception are cleared; in the second, a serpent (of form) folds himself around the rock to contain, in the third chamber, the interior imaginative expansion which occurs within the containing form; in the fourth chamber raging lions of fire melt metals, which are 'cast' in the fifth 'into the expanse' of imaginative form and received, in the sixth chamber, as books which are then arranged in libraries. Among other things, this section gives a visionary account of Blake's aesthetics. In the popular mind, visions are usually confused with hallucinations, and Blake was forever being asked silly questions like 'where' did he see his visions, to which he on at least one occasion replied by tapping his forehead.[13] The printing house in hell shows the process of expansion from within to the infinite, in an inversion of the Newtonian space of the corporeal world, an 'opening of a centre', as Blake calls it elsewhere, that occurs inside not merely a rock but a rock around which is coiled a viper to make the space doubly constricted. But the imaginative expansion which occurs within the enclosed space that is hollowed out of the rock is by no means formless. The 'unnamed forms' that cast the molten metals into the expanse in the fifth chamber are unnamed because they are imaginative forms for which ordinary names do not apply; but they are not for that reason vague or blurry. Blake's ideal in pictorial art is 'the wiry bounding line' without which art becomes chaos, and visionary art more than any other had to be minutely discriminated:

The great and golden rule of art, as well as of life, is this: That the more distinct, sharp, and wiry the bounding line, the more perfect the work of art; and the less keen and sharp, the greater is the evidence of weak imitation, plagiarism, and bungling. . . . Leave out this l[i]ne and you leave out life itself; all is chaos again, and the line of the almighty must be drawn out upon it before man or beast can exist.[14]

The fifth expository section attacks the monistic idea that denies any kind of duality and develops the doctrine of the contraries in dividing being into 'the Prolific', which is active, and 'the Devouring', which is passive. The Devouring half of existence thinks it is in power: 'to the devourer it seems as if the producer was in his chains, but it is not so, he only takes portions of existence and fancies that the whole.' Both are necessary, and both must retain their identities: 'These two classes of men are always upon earth, & they should be enemies; whoever tries to reconcile them seeks to destroy existence.' Blake's doctrine wants to 'marry' the two but not to destroy their individuality and synthesize them. Religion, he says, wants to do this and hence seeks to destroy existence: 'Religion is an endeavour to reconcile the two.'

The fourth 'memorable fancy' is the boisterous satiric climax of *The Marriage*, for Swedenborg in this section is due for devastating and rough treatment indeed. It is an altogether astonishing performance as some extremely complex ideas are expressed in a scene of robust, and sometimes gruesome, humour. This section is based on the prospects of two 'eternal lots': that envisaged for the narrator by the pious Swedenborgian angel and that envisaged for the angel by the narrator. The first is a descent into a hell as seen by the angel, and the second is a brief space odyssey into empty abstract space, a sort of cosmic balloon flight, with Swedenborg's volumes literally as ballast.

The angel is horrified at the ideas presented in *The Marriage* thus far and warns the narrator that he is preparing himself for a 'hot burning dungeon', whereupon the narrator suggests that they show each other their eternal lots. The angel takes him through a stable (of 'the horses of instruction') and a church into the church vault and down a winding cavern to a nether void, where they finally sit in the roots of an oak, the angel being suspended upside down in a fungus. The view of the abyss which emerges by degrees from the smoke is a parody of a Swedenborgian view of hell. But suddenly there appears a monstrous serpent with streaks of green and purple 'like those on a tygers forehead'. It comes 'to the east, distant about three degrees'—which is to say from Paris, which as Blake knew from his engravings of geographical books, was three degrees in longitude from London—and the angel sees it as Leviathan and departs in terror. The whole scene, being a projection of the angel's 'metaphysics', changes to a peaceful one with the sound of a harper when the angel leaves. The angel's view of the narrator's eternal lot miscarried in the appearance of the revolutionary tiger-like creature from the east. For this lot, far from being eternal, was very much subject to change. The harper sings a song on the theme of one of the proverbs of hell, 'The man who never alters his opinion is like standing water, & breeds reptiles of the mind', like the one just seen.

The narrator finds the angel again and proposes to show the angel his lot. The angel laughs but is seized by force in the balloon ascent through a cosmic scheme (that may have come from Boehme) to an abstract void, where they see the same stable and church and altar with a bible, which, now opened, shows a deep pit. They descend into it, the narrator driving the angel before him, and enter one of seven brick houses ('the seven churches of Asia'). The humour now turns gruesome in the spectacle of 'a number of monkeys, baboons, & all of that species chaind by the middle, grinning and snatching at one another, but witheld by the shortness of their chains'. But some were able to reach others, and 'then the weak were caught by the strong and with a grinning aspect, first coupled with & then devoured, by plucking off first one limb and then another till the body was left a helpless trunk. this after grinning & kissing it with seeming fondness they devourd too'. Returning, the narrator brings a skeleton, which in the mill 'was Aristotles Analytics'. The angel tries to shame the narrator, and he in turn replies that it is a waste of time to 'converse with you whose works are only Analytics'.

In the following expository section, Swedenborg is formally read out of the company of visionaries—if that was necessary after his space trip. And he is identified as a writer of 'analytics': 'Thus Swedenborgs writings are a recapitulation of all superficial opinions, and an analysis of the more sublime, but no further.'

The last 'memorable fancy', and the end of *The Marriage* proper, first presents a debate between an angel and devil, which the devil begins by announcing Blake's religion of man and God. The angel turns blue with horror but mastering his feelings turns yellow and as last 'pink and smiling', as he replies with the idea that God is one, visible in Christ, and that Christ sanctioned the ten commandments, all other men being 'fools, sinners, & nothings'. The devil shows then that Christ himself broke all the commandments, but that 'Jesus was all virtue, and acted from impulse. not from rules'. At this, the angel and devil embrace and emerge as Elijah. The contraries are now married, and the angel-devil has become the narrator's friend. They read the bible in its 'infernal' (visionary) sense together, and the narrator (Blake) announces his 'Bible of

Hell: which the world shall have whether they will or no'. The whole work ends with the maxim: 'One Law for the Lion & Ox is Oppression', not quite another proverb of hell but rather the necessary postulate for freedom within which the contraries can work.

Appended to *The Marriage* is 'A Song of Liberty', in twenty numbered statements with an exultant shout that 'Empire is no more!' and a 'chorus' celebrating the holiness of life. This song furnishes a bridge between *The Marriage* and *America: A Prophecy*, making an apocalyptic application of the general doctrine of *The Marriage* in the political context of *America*, with some elements added.

Swedenborg may have been the proximate object of the satire in *The Marriage*, and the bouncing around he gets in it certainly provides most of the fun. But Blake's varied exposition of the contraries which furnish being with its essential vitality and his idea of the expanded sense-perception necessary to perceive—and hence to know, since for Blake knowledge is 'immediate by sense'—makes *The Marriage* much more than satire. He will later make modifications in his idea of the contraries, making the pink and smiling angelic hinderers of positive act genuinely satanic; but the basic ontological doctrine of a polar being continues in his later work.

5 | Political prophecies

While he was writing and engraving the prophetic lyrics of *Experience* and the revolutionary manifesto of *The Marriage*, Blake wrote for the radical publisher, Joseph Johnson, his most explicit political prophecy, *The French Revolution*. It was not to be one of his illuminated books but an ordinary book to be put out in letterpress by a publisher, the only one he ever wrote under these auspices. It is a pity that it was never published, for, as Erdman remarks of it, 'In this work, imaginatively high-flown as it was, he came closer than he ever would again to making his interpretation of history comprehensible to the English public of his own day'.[1] It was set in type but not printed, and the only copy we have is a single set of proofs.

Why it was never published remains obscure. To be sure, Johnson drew back from publishing Thomas Paine's *Rights of Man* in 1791, the date given on the title-page of *The French Revolution*, but he was willing to publish an abridgement of Paine's work. But Priestley's home was ransacked by a mob opposed to his liberal principles in 1791, and Blake, who described one of the political prisoners in the Bastille as being 'confined for a writing prophetic', perhaps sensed by the time the work was to appear that free speech at home might be seriously abridged and withdrew it himself in the 'nervous fear' he later mentioned to his friend Flaxman. The subtitle of the *French Revolution* announced it to be in 'seven books', and the advertisement said 'the remaining books are finished, and will be published in their order', but no others have survived. Very likely there were no others, for Blake was forever announcing grand plans and then cutting back (like the twelve books of *Milton*, which reduced to two). Perhaps nervous fear not only prompted him to withdraw what he had written but prevented him from

85

writing more. He would go on to write *America: A Prophecy*, dated 1793, but its events, though American leaders are mentioned by name, are there raised to a safer prophetic level; George III is not mentioned by name, and the American war did not suggest the kinds of analogies suggested by the revolution across the channel. In the future Blake's political allegory would be there, but so obscurely that some critics can deny its very existence.

The representation of events in France from 19 June, from the assembly of the three estates and the resolution of the commons not to disband until they had given France a constitution, to 15 July when the troops surrounding the city were dispersed after the fall of the Bastille, are prophetically heightened, and partly invented to make a good drama, but they are not obscure. Blake avails himself of the dramatist's license to change the location from Versailles to Paris, so the citizen in the street can look up to the building in which the commons were meeting and the Bastille can be felt as a presence. And he creates a couple of nobles for the king's council, the proceedings of which he has to imagine since they were not published.[2] But, as the French critic, Pierre Berger, remarked, his characters though symbolic 'are even historically true in their chief features, and it is mere justice to recognize that Blake has given them the characters which they had in the popular imagination and which they have kept in history'.[3]

But of imaginative heightening there is a good deal. The king descends to his council to the accompaniment of thunder, and deep tremours shake the nation:

> . . . shady mountains
> In fear, utter voices of thunder; the woods of France embosom the
>   sound;
> Clouds of wisdom prophetic reply, and roll over the palace roof
>   heavy.
>
> . . .
>
> For the Commons convene in the Hall of the Nation. France shakes!

The governor of the Bastille howls as he listens to the terrors when he stalks from tower to tower, now given names like Horror, Darkness, Bloody, Order, Destiny, and Tower of God, each holding prisoners whose crimes are specified. As the king begins his council meeting, he looks out of his window to his army:

... from the window he saw his vast armies spread over the hills,
Breathing red fires from man to man, and from horse to horse;
then his bosom
Expanded like starry heaven, he sat down: his Nobles took their
ancient seats.

The debate that follows represents the various factions among the
nobles. The Duke of Burgundy speaks for the *ancien régime*, asking,
'Shall this marble built heaven' of noble privilege 'become a clay
cottage' and 'these mowers / From the Atlantic mountains [America]
mow down all this great starry harvest of six thousand years?' The
popular finance minister Necker is accused and exiled by the king,
as he actually was. The Archbishop of Paris fears for ecclesiastical
privilege and counsels the use of troops. Orléans, 'generous as
mountains', asks 'can Nobles be found when the people are free',
and is followed by the Abbé de Sieyès, who counsels the nobles to
'Hear, O Heavens of France, the voice of the people, arising from
valley and hill', and urges the removal of the troops. After a few
more speeches, the troops are commanded to leave, Burgundy
giving the king's command and Fayette (Lafayette) carrying it out.
The work ends with the 'Senate in peace' sitting 'beneath morning's
beam'.

The removal of the troops actually took place on 15 July, and
before that the Bastille was stormed. Though the destruction of
this political prison was essential in Blake's mind, he rearranges
events to make the removal of the troops and the capitulation of
the king precede its destruction, which is not even mentioned.
Blake sees violence as the 'accident' of revolution and not its 'substance', to use one of his favourite distinctions, and the important
event here is not the destruction of the prisons but the capitulation
of the king and nobles, a change of mind which they are shown as
being persuaded to make, though reluctantly, rather than being
forced to it by physical means. This in 1790, when Blake finished
the first book of his poem, could be seen as a step, in the political
context, toward apocalypse, which to him was indeed a change of
mind on a large scale.

The French Revolution follows actual events closely enough so
that the changes Blake introduced can be specifically noted. In
America: A Prophecy, which he probably worked on from 1791 to
the title-page date of 1793, the level of *mimesis* moves higher.
Though the historical Americans appear in this work by name,

King George III becomes, in the final version, 'The Guardian Prince of Albion'; and a very active character in the conflict who makes his first full appearance here is Orc. *America* might be thought of as similar to a tone-poem. Blake has, as Erdman has shown, a fairly specific 'programme' in mind in this work, but the work itself, rather than following specific events, has a narrative structure that derives more from the 'prophetic' meaning of those events, as seen in the controlling image of a pestilence and in the emergence of the vital form of the revolutionary Orc in the Atlantic, as well as in the spiritual solidarity of the Americans. The Americans win the war without firing a single shot. Specific events can be seen in the overall action—and some of the details would have been more readily noticeable by Blake's contemporaries than they are by us.

For *America* is a 'prophecy', as the subtitle says, in Blake's sense of the term, with which modern biblical scholars would agree. A prophecy is not a prediction. *America* could hardly predict events that had occurred a decade earlier. 'Prophets', in the predictive sense of the term, says Blake, 'have never existed. Jonah was no prophet in the modern sense, for his prophecy of Nineveh failed' because the Ninevites reformed.[4] The prophet in Blake's sense sees with imaginative vision in the light of eternal principles. Isaiah and Ezekiel were prophets not because they predicted events but because, seeing imaginatively, they saw more deeply and clearly than other men. As far as predicting the future is concerned, 'Every honest man is a Prophet; he utters his opinion both of private & public matters. Thus: If you go on So, the result is So. He never says, such a thing shall happen let you do what you will'.[5] In a very real sense, of course, *America* does show that if Albion's Guardian Prince goes on so, the result will be as it was in the American war, and hence a sort of prediction is made. Blake makes the cosmic implications of the action clear by showing an analogue between the American war and Edward III's war in France in the fourteenth century, and he uses the plague of 1348 that followed that war as a controlling image in his prophetic account of the American one. But here the plague is not a consequence of the war; it is the weapon by means of which the Guardian Prince of Albion tries to subdue the rebellious Americans. And the weapon of this visionary form of bacteriological warfare backfires; for the plague is turned back by Orc in the Atlantic, and by the spiritual solidarity of the Americans' rushing together, to infect Albion itself and shake not only the Prince's authority but also the thrones of all Europe—as well as starting a sexual revolution.

America is one of the most accessible of Blake's prophecies if the action is seen as occurring on a huge stage, or screen, extending from England across the Atlantic to the coast of America, with all characters simultaneously present. The 'Preludium', however, is not so accessible, because Blake combines in it some of the political themes of the prophecy and elements of a mythology that is by no means yet worked out into any kind of coherent form.

The preludium as a formal feature is common in music, where, historically, the praeludium or prelude was a rather free prefatory composition preceding a longer one—at least until the nineteenth century when Chopin and others wrote preludes that were entirely independent. The Preludium to the *Book of Urizen* is actually an argument announcing the subject and invoking the muse. But in *America* and *Europe* they play thematically with the works that follow, giving a kind of framework for them. The Preludium to *America* describes 'the shadowy daughter of Urthona' standing 'before red Orc', bringing him food in iron baskets and cups. She wears a helmet and carries a quiver of pestilential arrows but is naked, though 'clouds roll around her loins'. She is silent, unable to speak. Orc, who is now fourteen, tells her that, though her stern father had chained him, his spirit soars and takes various forms. He is feeble in his caverns but when she brings him food he says, 'I howl my joy! and my red eyes seek to behold they face'; but he cannot see through the clouds. Yet he rends the links of his chain and 'Round the terrific loins he siez'd the panting struggling womb; / It joy'd: she put aside her clouds & smiled her first-born smile'. Then she knows him as 'the image of God who dwells in darkness of Africa' and knows 'thou are fall'n to give me life in regions of dark death'. She feels him on her American plains, sees him in a serpent in Canada, an eagle in Mexico, a lion in Peru, and a whale in the South-sea. All these manifestations of Orc are associated with North and South America, even that in Africa because of American slavery. And in context it is clear that politically the liberation of Orc from his chains is connected with revolts of one kind or another. Though at fourteen he is just pubescent, his sexual union with the shadowy female marks a coming to maturity of a new force. His soaring spirit has been on her American plains all along; but now it will become effective, as it was not before.

The action in the Preludium stirs up other resonances, some rather confused. Though the sexual union has fulfilled the shadowy female and taken her out of the state in which she automatically or instinctively fed Orc without consciousness of either his or her identity, it remains ambiguous. Her coming to consciousness is painful:

> O what limb rending pains I feel. thy fire & my frost
> Mingle in howling pains, in furrows by thy lightnings rent.

Literally, of course, the pains can be those of childbirth. But the process being described is not one of life but of death: 'This is eternal death; and this the torment long foretold.' The emergence of Orc and his union with the female, while it brings about a movement for freedom, also brings about at another level a fall into the different tyranny of the cycle of nature. This is reinforced, I think, in the phrase, ' that dread day when Orc assay'd his fierce embrace'; for 'that dread day' becomes for Blake almost a shorthand reference in *The Four Zoas* to the beginning of the disintegration of Albion, unfallen humanity, into his component warring natures. And it is not quite clear whether her arrows are pestilential ones; or whether she merely has a bow like that used to shoot such arrows; or whether she is reborn without the helmet, arrows, and bow.

The preludium was added to *America*. It was not an original part of it, and some of its convoluted symbolism may result from Blake's having begun to develop his cast of symbolic characters in a new direction, to be seen in the first systematic presentation of the myth of the Fall in *The Book of Urizen*. It is also true that in the earliest and latest issues of *America*, the preludium included four rather disillusioned lines, to follow the end:

> The stern Bard ceas'd, asham'd of his own song; enrag'd he swung
> His harp aloft sounding, then dash'd its shining frame against
> A ruin'd pillar in glittring fragments; silent he turn'd away,
> And wander'd down the vales of Kent in sick & drear lamentings.

The bard is not ashamed in the prophecy itself. The Guardian Prince of Albion burns in his nightly tent, and his fires pierce the souls of warlike Americans—Washington, Franklin, Paine, Warren, Gates, Hancock, and Greene, who assemble. Washington speaks and warns them of war and oppression. Albion's prince, now shown to have a dragon form, continues to glare at the Americans. Suddenly in the Atlantic Orc emerges, 'Intense! naked! a Human fire fierce glowing, as the wedge / Of iron heated in the furnace'. The 'King of England'—identified thus only once—trembles, as a voice announces a resurrection that ends with the closing motto of 'A Song of Liberty' from *The Marriage*: 'For Empire is no more, and now the Lion & Wolf shall cease'. Albion's Angel, the god of royalty, Urizen, then asks the fierce human form whether he is not Orc, 'Blasphemous Demon, Antichrist, hater of Dignities', and Orc replies that 'times are ended; . . . morning gins to break' and that Urizen's law of the ten commandments is to be stamped to dust. The apocalypse is at hand. The Prince of Albion calls on his colonial governors, his 'thirteen angels', to go to war. Boston's Angel cries out that he will no longer obey, and soon all the others throw off their robes of authority and rush to grovel at Washington's feet. The British soldiers, in a line that recalls the fifth stanza of 'The Tyger', 'sent up a howl / Of anguish: threw their swords & muskets to the earth'. But Albion's Angel musters diseases, 'plagues obedient to his voice', and sends them on America. America would have been lost but 'all rush together in the night in wrath and raging fire', and the plagues are sent back to England, 'driven by flames of Orc'. As a result, the British soldiers in England 'cast their swords & spears to earth, & stood a naked multitude'. The religious powers hide, and so does the poet-laureate, as political and sexual liberation come together, the priests rushing for cover 'Leaving the females naked and glowing with the lusts of youth'. 'The Heavens' of repression are melting, and Urizen, weeping above them, sends down snows to hide the fires of Orc. The prophecy ends with the shaking of Europe's thrones, as the bands of Albion, sick from their own plagues, go to shut the gates of their 'law-built heaven', which have been burned open.

In *America* and its Preludium Blake introduces into his work for the first time by name Orc and Urizen, as active participants, and incidentally Urthona and Enitharmon, all of whom become important as his visionary universe of symbolic characters develops. In the *French Revolution* there was no mythological machinery at all, the account of historical events being raised to a prophetic level by extremely active poetic imagery. But in *America* events occur at the level of history with actual historical characters, like George Washington, and at another level at which historical characters take on supernatural characteristics, like the burning Prince of Albion, who is at once George III and a burning reptilian form. But there is also another level of participant in the revolutionary Orc and Urizen, imaginative personified forms of human forces and impulses. Since from this point onwards Blake's prophecies will shift their focus to deal directly with these characters and others like them, assimilating concrete events to the total imaginative form of the interrelationships of the actions of his myth, it might be well to take stock of their development in 1793, just before Blake begins to systematize them, and to add some additional important characters, in *The Book of Urizen* and after.

Blake has the habit of dropping his reader into his unfamiliar imaginative universe very much *in medias res*, without any clue as to what his strange personages are or where they came from. The central character Los, the prophetic spirit, is first introduced in the midst of a cosmic mess produced by Urizen's attempt to create a solid world by the simple words, 'And Los, round the dark globe of Urizen / Kept watch', with no suggestion as to who he is or why he should keep watch. Blake does not believe in what in the theatre are called 'pointed entrances'. This is rather maddening at first; but it really turns out to be the best way, for entering this visionary universe requires an imaginative leap, not an easy ascent, and even a little explanation might well run the risk of inviting literal allegorical equations which would vitiate the whole enterprise.

When the 'shadowy daughter of Urthona' stands before 'red Orc', we are not starting at the beginning, for Orc has been chained by her father 'stern abhorr'd'. In the Prophecy itself, Albion's Angel asks Orc if he is 'not Orc, who . . . / Stands at the gate of Enitharmon to devour her children'. The angel sees everything as distorted by good and evil, of course, but he knows Orc by reputation at least, and somewhere in the story there is a character named Enitharmon, though we are told nothing about her. Urizen makes his first appearance toward the end of the Prophecy—though he is more sharply delineated in another work contemporary with *America, Visions of the Daughters of Albion*.

In *America* Orc looms very large in importance, and, though he has like Blake's tiger a fearful component, he is in his Promethean energy an apocalyptic force that will destroy the political form of error. Blake has not yet introduced Los, who as the prophetic spirit presides over and to some extent brings about the apocalypses of the later works; and in *America* Los's function seems not to be needed, being absorbed in Orc. Orc, as a principle needed to oppose and overthrow Urizen, seems extremely important in the context of the explicitly political prophecies; but as the visionary characters are developed, he loses importance and takes on more fully those negative features that are seen even at his first appearance. His direct opposition to Urizen continues in the cyclical pattern of history, which moves through alternating periods of oppression and revolt, and in Blake's optimistic view these cycles spiral toward a final apocalypse; but Orc turns out to be inadequate. When Blake devised the grand scheme of the 'four zoas', (the aspects of man represented in their unfallen and fallen states in the work so titled, Orc becomes the fallen version of Luvah and a potent but rather destructive force associated with nature. His emanation or female counterpart in that work turns out to be an adaptation of the 'nameless shadowy female' of the Preludium now identified as Vala, embodying the tyranny of the natural process, the cycle, in Eliot's phrase, of 'birth, copulation, and death', which Blake called 'the female will'. In *Milton*, and after, Orc is largely dropped.

The opposition of Orc and Urizen was probably the root conception of Blake's myth, and in this Urizen may have come first as a character needed to represent the false god of this world who was worshipped by materialist religion. An early version, dating from about 1789, is Tiriel, the aged and insane tyrant of the MS work of that title for which Blake made illustrations but never engraved. In 'Tiriel', which tells the last part of a much longer story implied in the narrative, the aged king, who had overthrown his father and mother Har and Heva long since and ruined his children, comes home to die after a period of wandering like Lear's. Blake later uses pieces of this story for allusion in, and for the setting of, *The Book of Thel*; but little more. His other version of Urizen is his comically reductive version of the god of the 'religious' whom he calls 'Nobodaddy', or nobody's father, as John Sampson pointed out long ago.[6] His character of Nobodaddy owes something to Swift's *On the Mechanical Operation of the Spirit*, in its reduction of spirit to wind in a MS poem beginning 'Let the Brothels of Paris be opened':

> Then old Nobodaddy aloft
> Farted & belchd & coughd
> And said I love hanging & drawing & quartering
> Every bit as well as war & slaughtering[.][7]

But a comic parody of a god like Nobodaddy would hardly do
to reveal the inadequacies of the god worshipped by the churches.
In some moods Blake saw the god of the churches as indeed a
'sky-god' who was taken as sanctioning if not actually enjoying the
things Nobodaddy loves. But only a real fool could worship
Nobodaddy, and Blake had no interest in fools. He needed a figure
who was at once believably recognizable as the abstract god of the
'religious', as actually worshiped, but also one who could be shown
to be a false god. So he created Urizen. Urizen is often hopelessly—
and even comically—inept, but he is a complex figure despite that,
embodying, as one of the Zoas of man's nature, his rational faculty
as it works apart from the other aspects of man's nature and also
embodying the kinds of spiritual projections that might be made by
that nature. In *America* Urizen is shown as almost pitifully in-
competent to deal with the fires of Orc, as Blake, exultant with
hopes for the overthrow of oppression, there represents him. But a
year later Urizen appears in the frontispiece to *Europe* as the Ancient
of Days, by which title this picture is best known. And, while the
bearded figure closed up in a tight sphere stabbing down into the
abyss with compasses to draw a circle on the infinite is not the god
whom man's imagination will bring him to, the figure has tremendous power and grandeur. It is not a merely satiric portrait.
Indeed, it was one of Blake's favourite pictures, and he spent some
time on his death bed colouring a copy of it. The figure of Urizen
modulates considerably in his work—in *Milton* he gets pretty flatly
identified as Satan—and he lends himself to modulation because he
is complex. Constant in his character is that impulse to know in
concrete material terms and to make things rational even at the
expense of missing the richer entanglements of human experience
that do not readily lend themselves to that kind of knowledge.
Readers of Blake quickly come to use the adjective 'Urizenic',
which is pejorative but not always devastatingly so: it is well to
keep context in mind all through Blake's work.

Urthona is in *America* merely mentioned as the archetypal father
oppressor or confiner. He is actually said to be the father of the
shadowy female, and, as she probably represents nature as well as
being specifically connected with the American continent, his name,
probably derived as an aptronymic (the word coined by Franklin P.
Adams) from earth-owner, would suggest something like an earth
spirit here. Later on Urthona, still connected with the earth, will

become the name for the unfallen Los and will appear usually in the ambiguous form of a 'spectre', a kind of character we shall have occasion to consider in *The Four Zoas*.

Enitharmon is also here only alluded to in *America*. In *Europe* she assumes considerable importance as a sort of malevolent Queen of Heaven, seeking female dominion, whose dream of eighteen centuries forms an important part of the poem. In the myth she is the emanation, or female counterpart, of Los. There, the character ranges from being a 'coy mistress' striving to dominate Los by coquetry to being 'an help meet' for him in building Golgonooza, the city of art, as a step toward achieving Jerusalem, the city of God.

I should like to return now to the political prophecies but instead of taking up *Visions of the Daughters of Albion*, produced in the same year as *America*, move ahead to *Europe*, which picks up where *America* left off and views the political situation of 1793 in the great frame of biblical history. *Europe* is an enormously rich and complex work, and all that will be possible here is a brief look at its overall structure. Ultimately it should be read with the help of Erdman's detailed account of the political allegory within its 'prophetic envelope'.[8] I should like here to focus a little more attention than is usually given on the difficult but important Preludium.

The work as a whole is prefaced with a delightful lyric touching on the theme of expanded sense-perception. A fairy is captured by the poet in his hat. The fairy, made 'tipsie' by cups of 'sparkling poetic fancies', sits on the poet's table and dictates *Europe*. The Preludium he dictates finds nature of the earlier Preludium now exhausted, discouraged by some of her progeny, but freed by the birth of Christ at the end, to return to her virgin state. It should be quoted in full:

> The nameless shadowy female rose from out the breast of Orc:
> Her snaky hair brandishing in the winds of Enitharmon;
> And thus her voice arose.
>
> O mother Enitharmon wilt thou bring forth other sons?
> To cause my name to vanish, that my place may not be found.
> For I am faint with travel!
> Like the dark cloud disburdend in the day of dismal thunder.
>
> My roots are brandish'd in the heavens. my fruits in earth beneath
> Surge, foam, and labour into life, first born & first consum'd!

Consumed and consuming!
Then why shouldst thou accursed mother bring me into life?

I wrap my turban of thick clouds around my lab'ring head;
And fold the sheety waters as a mantle round my limbs.
Yet the red sun and moon,
And all the overflowing stars rain down prolific pains.

Unwilling I look up to heaven! unwilling count the stars!
Sitting in fathomless abyss of my immortal shrine.
I sieze their burning power
And bring forth howling terrors, all devouring fiery kings.

Devouring & devoured roaming on dark and desolate mountains
In forests of eternal death, shrieking in hollow trees.
Ah mother Enitharmon!
Stamp not with solid form this vig'rous progeny of fires.

I bring forth from my teeming bosom myriads of flames.
And thou dost stamp them with a signet, then they roam abroad
And leave me void as death:
Ah! I am drown'd in shady woe, and visionary joy.

And who shall bind the infinite with an eternal band?
To compass it with swaddling bands? and who shall cherish it
With milk and honey?
I see it smile & I roll inward & my voice is past.

　　　She ceast & rolld her shady clouds
　　　　Into the secret place.

Myth, politics, religion, and sex are so intertwined here that it is impossible to separate them. The political situation as represented retrospectively in the Preludium of *America* was on the whole hopeful, for there the shadowy female was a nubile maiden symbolizing the North American continent, and she was sexually fulfilled and made fruitful by the fierce embrace of the revolutionary Orc. The Prophecy itself showed the results of that union in the victory of the Colonies, which, as we have seen, was accompanied by the beginnings of a revolution for sexual freedom, and by earthquake tremours shaking the thrones of Europe. In the Preludium of *Europe* the whole situation has deteriorated badly. The shadowy female has now changed from the nubile virgin into a Medusa with 'snaky hair': to look on nature now is to turn into the stone of a solid material hell, or, to use Blake's later term, 'Ulro'. For nature has been subverted. It seems to me that the third stanza in particular

3. Plate from *The Book of Urizen*

4. Title-page from the uncoloured version of *Jerusalem*

shows this and also makes a specific allusion to a particular philosophical and political subversion of nature in Burke's *Reflections on
the Revolution in France*. Erdman has shown that Burke and Pitt
appear in the Prophecy itself, as Palamabron and Rintrah—or,
rather, as perverted versions of those figures.[9] Even Blake, who all
his life attacked 'natural religion' and 'natural man', could find the
philosophical and political inferences drawn from nature in the
thought underlying the Declaration of Independence acceptable,
and the embodiment of nature in the earlier shadowy female could
be optimistic. But in the reaction to revolution epitomized in
Burke's *Reflections*, nature had been debased. Burke derives the
principle of inheritance from the genetic, or as Blake would say
the 'sexual', aspect of nature, and inheritance is the basic principle
justifying continuation of the established order. An 'inheritable
crown; and inheritable peerage; and an house of commons and a
people inheriting privileges, franchises, and liberties, from a long
line of ancestors', says Burke, 'is the happy effect of following
nature', which he goes on to define as 'wisdom without reflection,
and above it'.[10] Inheritance from the model of nature is a 'sure
principle of conservation, and a sure principle of transmission',
which admits of improvement but no discontinuities. Burke does
not mention that presumably it also admits of deterioration. Blake
consistently symbolized an inherited crown and an inherited peerage
as heavens and stars. When, therefore, the shadowy female of the
Preludium says her 'roots are brandish'd in the heavens', it seems
to me that he has Burke's nature philosophy specifically in mind.
The proper fruits of nature, as she was shown in the earlier Preludium, are driven underground 'in earth beneath' and have to
struggle to arise from their caverns, as did the imprisoned Orc,
only to be consumed.

In the next two stanzas, II. 12-19, Blake has introduced a parody
of the immaculate conception, with a debased nature being im-
pregnated by an abstract starry heaven. The passage is obscure.
Later, in *Jerusalem*, Blake would forthrightly reject the immaculate
conception, but here he is a bit more cautious. Nature here has
become merely genetic and needs to teem, though wanting to
avoid it. Discouraged by the whole process, she hides her 'lab'ring
head'—not her loins because even sex has been subverted by
Urizenic religion—but she is compelled to 'look up to heaven'.
She does so from an 'immortal shrine', appropriate to a religion

D

that exalts physical 'sexual' nature and idolizes the female principle in the chivalric code eulogized by Burke, who thought that naturally 'woman is but an animal; and an animal not of the highest order' but she should be exalted as a queen, or as an object of chivalric adoration, to support 'manly sentiment and heroic enterprize' and preserve the established order.[11] The shadowy female says of the starry heavens, 'I sieze their burning power'. But—and here Blake brings in one of the reversals of intention he loves so well—the progeny are not starry kings but 'howling terrors', rather resembling Orc, which, to allegorize a little, suggests that even this kind of union of spirit and matter produces spirits who, instead of supporting kings, are all spirits 'devouring fiery kings'. The concept of the union of spirit and flesh contains within it a revolutionary principle.

But the howling terrors thus produced are subject to subversion, to being given 'solid form' by the tyrannical Enitharmon. And the shadowy female complains when Enitharmon stamps them with her signet. This passage suggests the loss of revolutionary nerve on the part of some who were sympathetic to the American revolution but who pulled back from the revolution in France. Even Burke himself had urged conciliation of the Colonies—though his motive was not independence for the Colonies but the preservation of the empire.

But in the midst of complaining to Enitharmon, the shadowy female feels 'visionary joy' as she becomes aware of the birth of another infant, 'the infinite'. And she asks in a series of questions which are not answered except by a smile, 'who shall bind the infinite with an eternal band?' Clearly not Enitharmon. And at this point nature retires, as it were, to resume her earlier virgin status:

> I see it smile & I roll inward & my voice is past.
>
>> She ceast & rolld her shady clouds
>> Into the secret place.

The climactic event of the nativity of Christ in the Preludium leads directly into the Prophecy itself, which begins by evoking in its opening lines Milton's 'Ode on the Morning of Christ's Nativity:

>> The deep of winter came;
>> What time the secret child,
> Descended thro' the orient gates of the eternal day:

As in the Ode, 'War ceas'd, & all the troops like shadows fled to their abodes'. But Blake has changed the nativity to morning, and the scene quickly alters to night, as the sons and daughters of Enitharmon gather in her 'crystal house'. Milton's Ode invokes the 'crystal spheres' to make music in the thirteenth stanza of his Ode, and a musical celebration occurs in Blake's poem. But the word 'crystal' is somewhat ominous, because it often symbolizes in Blake the 'sexual' dominion of the female will, however lovely and clear. It appears in this sense not only in a late MS poem, 'The Crystal Cabinet', but also in *The Four Zoas*. Los 'joy'd in the peaceful night' and told his sons that 'strong Urthona', no longer 'stern, abhorr'd' as he was in the Preludium to *America*, 'takes his rest'; and Urizen who 'glows like a meteor' as Blake's version of Lucifer is in the north, where he ought to be. He calls for loud music, not from the spheres, but from 'elemental strings', music that would 'Awake the thunders of the deep', and wake 'the shrill winds' until 'all the sons of Urizen look out and envy Los'. He seems to think that permanent peace and joy have come. In the Ode, Milton had said that if the 'ninefold harmony' of the 'angelic symphony' celebrating Christ's birth could continue, the golden age would be at hand:

> For, if such holy song
> Enwrap our fancy long,
> Time will run back and fetch the Age of Gold;
> . . .
>
> And Hell itself will pass away,
> And leave her dolorous mansions to the peering day.

But he adds that 'wisest Fate says No', that Christ must suffer on the cross to redeem us; but, before we are to be redeemed, 'The wakeful trump of doom must thunder through the deep.'

Critics differ as to who speaks this passage, and such disagreement arises because often Blake does not indicate speakers by punctuation. Editors who punctuate Blake's text, like the late Sir Geoffrey Keynes, must make decisions about such matters; they often do so without warning that there may be problems. It is worthwhile to consult at points like this the literal text, with Blake's own scanty punctuation, edited by David Erdman and produced with help from a whole team of Blake scholars, including Sir Geoffrey Keynes himself. If the passage mentioned is read as a jubilant song of Los,

as Bloom reads it and as it seems to me it ought to be read, Los's
song becomes ironic in the extreme, for then he is the only one who
thinks that peace has come.[12] And there is a shock when he calls on
Orc to 'Arise':

> And we will crown thy head with garlands of the ruddy vine;
> For now thou art bound;
>   And I may see thee in the hour of bliss, my eldest born.

Orc does arise, but as a 'horrent Demon', 'surrounded with red
stars of fire, / Whirling about in furious circles round the immortal
fiend', Urizen, hardly in the mood that Los had in mind.

At this point Enitharmon, far from celebrating the era of peace
with Los, goes to Orc and sings her song of female dominion:

> Now comes the night of Enitharmons joy!
> Who shall I call? Who shall I send?
> That Woman, lovely Woman! may have dominion?
> Arise O Rintrah thee I call! & Palamabron thee!
> Go! tell the Human race that Womans love is Sin!
> That an Eternal life awaits the worms of sixty winters
> In an allegorical abode where existence hath never come:
> Forbid all Joy, & from her childhood shall the little female
> Spread nets in every secret path.

This is a speech not merely delighting in the prospect of female
dominion over man, as Blake saw it instanced in the medieval cult
of the coy virgin in the chivalric code. It is also a suppression of
female sexuality. Woman's love is a sin to women here. In the
Visions of the Daughters of Albion, which we shall take up shortly,
Blake celebrates female sexuality in a way that, again, makes him
very modern.

At this point Enitharmon goes to sleep for the eighteen hundred
years between the birth of Christ and 1793, dreaming of the
American revolution, among other things, and of the advent of
Newtonian science and druid temples:

> Then was the serpent temple form'd, image of infinite
> Shut up in finite revolutions, and man became an Angel;
> Heaven a mighty circle turning; God a tyrant crown'd.

The imagery is nightmarish, but she is pleased and smiles in her
sleep. Three times an angel attempts to blow the trump of doom—
symbolizing at the political level, as Erdman suggests, the three

imes Pitt tried to go to war with France—and finally 'a mighty
Spirit', who is Newton, blows it.[13] Enitharmon awakes, not know-
ng she wakes or even that she has slept, and picks up where she
eft off, calling on goddesses and women to help her cause, among
them Oothoon of *The Visions*: 'Why wilt thou give up womans
secrecy my melancholy child?' But her peace is shattered when she
calls up Orc to 'give our mountains joy of thy red light'. 'But
errible Orc'

> Shot from the heights of Enitharmon;
> And in the vineyards of red France appear'd the light of his fury.

The imagery is of war, and Enitharmon 'groans & cries in anguish
and dismay'. Los, 'with a cry that shook all nature to the utmost
pole', instead of the music with which he had hoped to shake it at
the beginning, calls his sons not to a celebration but 'to the strife
of blood'. The specific reference to France in this context used to
be taken to mean that Blake deplored the revolution there. But as
Erdman's close examination of historical allegory here shows, what
Blake is seeing as so bloody is not the revolution itself but the
counter-revolution in England's declaration of war on France.

Blake completed his prophetic survey of continents with the
Song of Los, dated 1795 on the title-page. *The Song of Los* is sub-
titled 'Africa, Asia' and is divided into two corresponding sections,
represented as having been sung by Los as a bard 'at the tables of
Eternity'. Africa begins with Adam and gives a condensed account
of the spiritual state of man through Noah's flood, the decalogue,
the beginning of the Christian era, Mohammud, Newton and
Locke, Rousseau and Voltaire, and ends with George III as 'The
Guardian Prince of Albion' burning in his 'nightly tent', as he was
at the beginning of *America*.

The Asia section picks up the story after *Europe*:

> The Kings of Asia heard
> The howl rise up from Europe!
> And each ran out from his Web;
> From his ancient woven Den;
> For the darkness of Asia was startled
> At the thick-flaming, thought-creating fires of Orc.

The kings cry in 'bitterness of soul' complaining about subversion
of the principles on which tyranny operates. Urizen hears and flies

over Europe to the place of Eden where Adam's bones lie bleached
and Urizen bellows his thunders. But Orc rises 'like a pillar of fire
above the Alps', and the dead arise in the apocalypse:

> The Grave shrieks with delight, & shakes
> Her hollow womb, & clasps the solid stem:
> Her bosom swells with wild desire:
> And milk & blood & glandous wine
> In rivers rush & shout & dance,
> On mountain, dale and plain.

At this 'Urizen Wept'.

The Song of Los thus supplies the prophetic framework to sur-
round the narratives of *America* and *Europe*, to put them in the
perspective of the whole spiritual history of man, and they complete
the cycle which begins in Eden and ends there.

Blake's view of race and colour, touched on earlier in connection
with 'The Little Black Boy', is succinctly stated in 'Africa':

> . . . Noah faded! black grew the sunny African
> When Rintrah gave Abstract Philosophy to Brama in the East:

As Kathleen Raine has suggested, Blake is probably thinking here
of Brahma's system of logic.[14] Abstract philosophy furnishes the
grounds for race, and turns Noah white and the African black,
Brahma and the races of the east presumably remain brown. Concerning the black African, Blake's view is that he is close to primordial man and has been in a sense protected from the encrustation
of fallen civilization—ironically—by the separation because of his
black skin and hence is more readily to be regenerated than the
white man. This is part of the meaning in 'The Little Black Boy',
in the boy's ability, to shade the little English boy from the heat of
the sun, (as God), till he can bear it. Not only does the black boy's skin
enable him to stand the heat of the natural sun, but he is also closer
to God because he has not fallen as far. In *Visions of the Daughters of
Albion*, Oothoon is stamped by a signet as one of the 'swarthy
children of the sun', but spiritually her limbs are 'snowy'.

To go back now to 1793, *Visions of the Daughters of Albion* also
combines sex and politics, or, more specifically, slavery. It is a work
compounded of several elements. The context, or sources from
which it grew, are the *Journal* of Captain Stedman, treating a revolt
of slaves in Surinam (for which Blake engraved illustrations after

Stedman's paintings) and 'Oithona: A Poem' in *The Poems of Ossian* 'Translated [composed] by James MacPherson, Esqu.,' in which a young woman is carried off and raped by the enemy of her lover and, when her lover returns to avenge her, enters the fight disguised as a young soldier in order to meet her death. Other elements enter into it as well. Thematically there are echoes of the *Book of Thel*, *Songs of Innocence and of Experience*, and there is an ironic structural echo from Spenser's espousal poems in the repeated refrain—ironic because no espousal occurs in *The Visions*, only a rape.

The action in the work consists of the rape of Oothoon by Bromion (a 'roarer' as the Greek root of his name suggests); the rejection of Oothoon by her beloved, Theotormon, because she has been raped and hence is spoiled for him; and then there are fairly long speeches by each of the principals. The work functions on two levels simultaneously. One is the moral-political one of slavery, and the other is the moral-sexual one of sexuality itself. Bromion commits not only a sexual rape but a human one as a slaver. And Theotormon is not only the male chauvinist who is stunned into inaction and despair because, in being despoiled by rape, Oothoon has become spoiled sexual merchandise: he is also the weak moralist who cannot really bring himself to see Oothoon the slave as being someone he can identify with as human. The relationships with slavery and Stedman's *Narrative* should be pursued in Erdman. I should like to confine myself to a few remarks about the sexual-moral level of the work.

Visions has been usually read as a celebration of free love, and it is that. But it is also, and I think more importantly, an eloquent plea for understanding female sexuality. Oothoon is physically restricted and thwarted, but she is a spiritually liberated woman. After suffering the rape, she calls down a Promethean punishment on herself, only to be rejected by Theotormon. She bitterly attacks Urizen, the god of both Theotormon and Bromion, and also attacks Theotormon's morality directly to him, becoming in the process able to speak more freely. She has suffered the most bestial form of sexuality, rape, and she is plunged farther into the bitterness of the world of Experience by Theotormon's rejection of her *because* she was raped. The pattern here is rather like that seen in 'The Chimney Sweeper' of *Innocence*, in which children are sold into chimney sweeping, are turned black by soot, and then despised as subhuman creatures because they are black.

The categories of Blake's moral philosophy and the sexual euphemisms of a recent age make it difficult to avoid a pun here, so we might as well accept it: Oothoon is in the first part of the work 'a woman of Experience', one who has known sex in a debased form and accepts the blame for it in asking for suffering. But she passes beyond this stage to achieve Innocence—as Thel could have done but did not. She is, somewhat like Thomas Hardy's Tess, 'a pure woman', though experienced. The 'ungenerated' Thel-like characters in this drama are Bromion and Theotormon, to whom sexual relationship is a kind of fantasy. They are imprisoned by their fantasies and as absorbed by them as pubescent boys are. Oothoon has, in a sense, become a mature woman who can see sexuality as a joy reflected in all of nature: 'where ever beauty appears / If in the morning sun I find it: there my eyes are fix'd / In happy copulation.' Bromion and Theotormon subscribe to Enitharmon's code that 'Woman's love is Sin'. Oothoon has been liberated from it. Again, as so often, Blake is peculiarly modern.

6 | The shorter prophecies

The Blakes lived in Lambeth for the decade 1790 to 1800, and that period, especially the first five years, was one of the most productive of his career. Most of the works by which he is best known were produced, or at least finished, there, including *Songs of Experience*, *The Marriage*, *Visions*, *America*, and *Europe*, which have been discussed in previous chapters. Blake gives Lambeth as the place of publication on the title-pages of *America* and *Europe* and also on a group of prophecies that are more general than political, including *The [First] Book of Urizen* (1794), *The Book of Ahania* (1795), *The Book of Los* (1795), and *The Song of Los* (1795). The works with Lambeth on the title-page are usually referred to as the 'Lambeth Prophecies'.

The prophecies of this group that are not explicitly political set forth in a curious form, a combination of the epic and biblical narrative, Blake's myth of the Fall. Several of the symbolic characters of the myth were employed in earlier works, as we have seen; but in these books is found the first systematic development of their relationships, which will be continued and greatly expanded in *The Four Zoas*. These books, giving an account of the creation, have points of contact with Genesis and Exodus of the Bible and probably form 'The Bible of Hell' which Blake said in *The Marriage* 'the world shall have whether they will or no'.[1] Of these *The [First] Book of Urizen* forms a narrative core and provides the best introduction to the overall structure of Blake's myth.

The word 'First' in the title in brackets was erased in some copies, and there never was a second book. It may be, again, that Blake started out with a grander plan than he finally felt like executing. Or he may have started out to parody the Bible, in which Genesis is called 'the first book of Moses', and then stopped when in *Urizen* his narrative went beyond his version of Genesis to Exodus. Blake's creation myth is shot through with irony. First of all, it shows that the creation of the material world, far from being the work for which God should be praised, is actually identical with the Fall. Secondly, the creation is not the work of God at all but of the demiurge, Urizen. Thirdly, it is not really even his work but the result of a sort of chain reaction which he merely began by trying to create a reality that is monolithic and solid. It is actually made for him, not by him, when Los providentially stops the disintegrating changes to save man from falling too far into a state of 'eternal death' from which regeneration would be impossible. Fourthly, the narrative shows that Urizen's attempt to form a substance of reality in which there were no contraries, and hence no creative conflict of the 'mental war', actually resulted in the creation of a world in which a destructive cyclical conflict was an essential feature, represented symbolically in the opposition of Urizen and Orc. And finally, Urizen's laws are shown to fail at once and, if they have any success at all, they have it from an oppressive 'net of religion' which is spun from his sorrow at their failure. Blake loved to have his philosophical and other enemies hoist themselves with their own petards (or infect themselves with their own plagues, as we saw in *America*)—as, 'Locke's Opinions of Words & their Fallaciousness are Artful Opinions & Fallacious also'; 'Thus Plato confutes himself'; in a mathematical world God will have 'to be excentric if he creates'. In attacking the idea that physical existence is real, he says that it is only an idea in 'the mind of a fool':

Mental Things are alone Real what is Calld Corporeal Nobody Knows of its dwelling Place it is in Fallacy & its Existence an Imposture Where is the Existence Out of Mind or Thought Where is it but in the Mind of a Fool.[2]

At the most general level, the theme of *Urizen* is that material existence is nothing but a wrong-headed metaphysical assumption which has tragic consequences for man; and Blake tried to expose it for what it is by mythic irony.

Urizen is one of the most profusely illustrated of Blake's works, having ten pages of design in a total of twenty-eight, all richly coloured. In any serious study of the work, it ought to be 'read'—experienced—in its full form as text and design, and this can be quite readily done in the Blake Trust facsimile, less satisfactorily in the inexpensive 1929 facsimile published by Dent. Taking in text and designs together is quite different from merely reading the text. Stopping narrative movement at one of the full page designs gives the effect of enormous expansion and produces a majestic structural rhythm for the work that greatly enhances its power. The designs stick in the mind's eye and are carried over into the text, making Urizen rather less pitiful than the satire in the text makes him out to be and hence deepening the satire.

The Preludium uses the epic formula to state the subject, 'Of the primeval Priests assum'd power', and invokes as the muse the society of Eternals introduced here, asked to

> Dictate swift winged words, & fear not
> To unfold your dark visions of torment.

Blake never makes very explicit who his Eternals are, or the Council of God they become in *The Four Zoas*, and this troubles some readers. And indeed there is a problem demographically; for, if Urizen withdraws from them and falls, as he does here, and Los and Orc are translated into his fallen world, then who is left in Eternity? From a literal point of view, Blake has a similar problem with Jesus later on, for He both assumes the character of a dying god but yet remains, in *The Four Zoas*, as having at the same time another identity that presides over the whole action. One explanation is available in Blake's distinction between 'individuals' and 'states' in which individuals appear. Milton is instructed, in the work bearing his name: 'Distinguish therefore States from Individuals in those States. / States Change: but Individual Identities never change nor cease.'[3] Though the aspects of man represented by Urizen, Los, Orc (and, later, Tharmas) fall by division from their unity in Albion, the total man, their fall in a way constitutes moving into another state and something of their identity as integral aspects of unfallen man is retained in Eternity. I realize that in saying this I may be blurring some distinctions that will be needed later on in the matter of states in *Milton*, because Urizen, Los, and Orc are not exactly states. But the idea of persistence of identity is useful to keep in mind. The clearest statement of it is in *Jerusalem* (plates 13-14):

> For every thing exists & not one sigh nor smile nor tear,
> One hair nor particle of dust, not one can pass away.

Jesus, of course, needs no such postulate to explain His manifold appearances, because the divine imagination encompasses everything there is; but the idea might simplify certain things. The Eternals as persistent identities in Eden or Eternity are, at any rate, a necessary invention to express the duality of unfallen and fallen life in the cosmic drama of Blake's myth. It should not matter greatly if we do not see them very clearly—though Blake does include a picture of them, as two bearded older figures and two younger ones, on plate 15 of *Urizen*, looking down on the globe of the fallen world.

Urizen opens with the Eternals having become aware of a 'shadow of horror', the work of Urizen. Urizen, like his work, is hidden and secret, since he has literally abstracted himself from the corrective company of his peers: '. . . unknown, abstracted / Brooding secret, the dark power hid.' In cutting himself off from the checks and balances of mental intercourse with the other Eternals, Urizen commits the initial error which will result in chaos and ultimately in the Fall.

He behaves in a manner consistent with isolation by making things 'Self-closd', as he himself is. He measures things by themselves, making the relative absolute:

> 2. Times on times he divided, & measur'd
>   Space by space in his ninefold darkness
>   Unseen, unknown! . . .

And his obscure creations already exhibit the signs of chaos, for 'changes appeard'; there were no changes like these in Eternity. 'A self-contemplating shadow' (like Aristotle's first mover), Urizen struggles in silence with the unstable elements of the corporeal world:

> 3. For he strove in battles dire
>   In unseen conflictions with shapes
>   Bred from his forsaken wilderness,
>   Of beast, bird, fish, serpent & element
>   Combustion, blast, vapour and cloud.

When he finally considers his creation to be complete, he breaks his silence and prepares for open revolt. Summoned by his shrill trumpet, the myriads of Eternity muster to see the horror displayed and to hear Urizen outline his activities and creed:

4. From the depths of dark solitude. From
    The eternal abode in my holiness,
    Hidden set apart in my stern counsels
    Reserv'd for the days of futurity,
    I have sought for a joy without pain,
    For a solid without fluctuation
    Why will you die O Eternals?
    Why live in unquenchable burnings?

He recounts how he has subdued the elements and how he has formed his laws:

6. Here alone I in books formd of metals
    Have written the secrets of wisdom
    The secrets of dark contemplation
    By fightings and conflicts dire,
    With terrible monsters Sin-bred:
    Which the bosoms of all inhabit;
    Seven deadly Sins of the soul.

7. Lo! I unfold my darkness: and on
    This rock, place with strong hand the Book
    Of eternal brass, written in my solitude.

8. Laws of peace, of love, of unity:
    Of pity, compassion, forgiveness.
    Let each chuse one habitation:
    His ancient infinite mansion:
    One command, one joy, one desire,
    One curse, one weight, one measure
    One King, one God, one Law.

Urizen's error is complete. His mysterious solitude has enabled him to seek the single-dimensioned and to misconceive fundamentally the nature of existence. He has come not only to see the flames of the creative mental war with the reductive vision of the materialist, as nothing but 'unquenchable burnings'; he has also come to view them with the moral vision of the orthodox, as evil or 'eternal death'. From his point of view of 'holiness', he sees the duality within every breast as the duality of good and evil, and he forms a set of laws to enforce strict conformity to the 'good' in every sphere. He has, in short, failed to see that the contraries are necessary to human life.

The wrath of the Eternals is aroused, and they separate Urizen's world from Eternity, directing flames at him, and he must toil in

anguish to give more form to his world of error so that it may the
better be separated, though it is still relatively a chaos. Following
this separation, Urizen passes into a state of death and becomes a
'clod of clay'. And all progress in the further creation of his world,
beyond that required to separate it from Eternity, now stops.

At this point Los, the prophetic spirit enters, who has been rent
from the side of Urizen and who must give form to chaos. Though
Urizen now lies dead, he cannot be so eternally, for eternal death is
impossible in existence as Blake conceives it. Urizen is now at the
extreme 'limit' of being, verging on non-entity and threatening
thereby to destroy existence.[4] Accordingly, Los is seized by a
cosmic fear for existence itself. Providentially associated with
Urizen, he must, somewhat like an efficient cause, fix the 'limits' of
Urizen's fall in order to preserve both Urizen and his world from
complete annihilation. But first Los must himself become a part of
this world, however incompletely:

> 12. Los howld in a dismal stupor,
>   Groaning! gnashing! groaning!
>   Till the wrenching apart [between him and Urizen] was healed[.]

This does not, however, completely unite him with Urizen ('. . .
the wrenching of Urizen heal'd not'); but because Los labours
under an eternal responsibility, he comes to have a relationship
with Urizen that is somewhat like that of a father's relationship
with a perverse and destructive child.

Thus, it is not Urizen but Los, who, impelled by a cosmic fear,
must complete the creation of the corporeal world. Until Los acts,
Urizen does not even exist, except as an obscure and unstable
identity:

> Cold, featureless, flesh or clay,
> Rifted with direful changes
> He lay in a dreamless night

> 14. Till Los rouz'd his fires, affrighted
>   At the formless unmeasurable death.

Los begins to fix and give form to the chaotic and formless changes
of Urizen's monstrous creation:

> 5. He watch'd in shuddring fear
>   The dark changes & bound every change
>   With rivets of iron & brass [.]

While Urizen tries to hide his changes, Los continues to bind them, creating the world of time, 'Numb'ring with links. hours, days & years'. Urizen's eternal mind, bounded now, loses its eternal wrath, which becomes a lake, a symbol in Blake for formlessness. And Los's work with Urizen's mind continues until it is enclosed in the shaggy prehistoric head of 'natural man': '. . . a roof shaggy wild inclos'd / In an orb, his fountain of thought.' Then, in an augmentation of the seven days of creation to seven woeful ages, Los gives a contracted and fallen physical form to Urizen himself, at the same time restricting his sense perceptions. In the first age, he forms his spine, 'Like the linked infernal chain', and his ribs, covering his 'nerves of joy' (his sense of touch). In the second age, he forms his heart (the organ of pity) and the physical nervous system. In the third, he forms his corporeal eyes. In the fourth, he forms corporeal ears, which aspired in hope but 'petrified / As they grew'. In the fifth age, Urizen's sense of smell is made to 'bent down to the deep'. In the sixth age Los creates animal thirst and hunger. In the seventh, finally, Urizen as a physical form becomes oriented in physical space:

12. Enraged & stifled with torment
    He threw his right Arm to the north
    His left Arm to the south
    Shooting out in anguish deep,
    And his Feet stampd the nether Abyss
    In trembling & howling & dismay.

At this point, Urizen's world, as it has been created by Los, is complete. But it is inert. Urizen himself is still in chains, and all his creatures lie dead; his world is indeed 'a solid without fluctuation'. To dramatize the idea that oppositions are necessary to any world whatever, Blake now proceeds to show that the animation, even of the corporeal one, can come about only after the introduction of Urizen's opposite, the irrepressible and truly unquenchably burning active negation, Orc.

Just as the creation of Urizen's world had come about through the proximate cause of Los's fear, its animation comes about through a process of division begun by a cosmic pity. Pity in Blake almost always implies division, for to him it is the emotion that divides by separating him who pities from him who is pitied. He saw with shrewd psychological insight that one who pities does not so much identify himself with the object of pity as congratulate himself on not being that object or associated with it. Pity is to him the false brotherhood of the professionally pious. To elevate pity to the status of a virtue, moreover, actually tends to bring about the condition in which it is applicable, through someone's misery. 'Pity would be no more,' he remarks in *Songs of Experience*, 'If we did not make somebody Poor'.⁵ Since Urizen's world is a world of division, and since, indeed, his pious morality exalts pity, it is ironically appropriate that the animation which will ultimately fill his world with misery should come about by means of that emotion on a cosmic scale.

The animation progresses through three stages, the first two through pity, and the last through jealousy, another divisive Urizenic emotion. In the first stage, Los pities Urizen, who is lying corporeal and bound in chains, causing Los himself to divide into a slightly lesser Los and Enitharmon, who is his 'emanation' (a divided self) and the first woman. In the second stage, Los also pities *her* and embraces her. Having been separated from the whole or eternal Los, she is in part a woman of this world, and the divided emotions of the coy mistress are her characteristic:

> He embrac'd her, she wept, she refus'd
> In perverse and cruel delight
> She fled from his arms, yet he followd[.]

Los then begets Orc, 'On his own divided image'. In the final stage, Orc grows, and Los, now acting in his fallen state, becomes jealous of him and binds him on to the mountain. As a result, the bound Orc cries, creating the tension which quickens Urizen and his world to life:

> 5. The dead heard the voice of the child
>   And began to awake from sleep
>   All things. heard the voice of the child
>   And began to awake to life.
>
> 6. And Urizen craving with hunger
>   Stung with the odours of Nature
>   Explor'd his dens around[.]

The creation is now complete and alive. But it is far from being of the simple nature that Urizen had envisaged, for in the conflict that will ensue between the raw vitality of Orc and Urizen's efforts to suppress this vitality, the fallen world necessarily embodies the very opposition which Urizen had set out by denying. The whole process of creation which Blake describes in the myth has been that of the construction of a disorganized and debased shadow of the eternal world of mind, a shadow which preserves the contrariety of Eternity, but does so in the dangerous and unstable form of negations. Thus the account of the creation given in *The Book of Urizen* shows that conflict or war is a necessary aspect of any existence whatever; but that, whereas this war is creative and mental in a mental world, in a corporeal world it is destructive and corporeal. And whereas the mental world can perceive this war in its true light as a necessary aspect of life, the corporeal world, with its bounded and limited perceptions, looks at conflict as something to be suppressed. But conflict can be suppressed only temporarily. Though Orc is now chained on the mountain, he will inevitably grow, as he did in the Preludium to *America*, and burst his chains to engage Urizen in combat. And though Urizen may put him down for a time, Orc will always rise again, with the result that Urizen's corporeal world will forever be engaged in cyclically recurring struggles. Thus, ironically, the corporeal world, and not Eternity, contains the life of 'unquenchable burnings'. 'The solid without fluctuation' and the 'joy without pain' are but phantoms of abstraction.

Though we know this, Urizen does not. As his actions in the rest of the book indicate, he continues to believe that a simple and solid world is possible, for he begins a survey of his creation with the idea of applying his laws, 'exploring his dens' with the science of lines and plummets. But Urizen thus exploring is a potential danger to what is left of vision in the corporeal world—represented by the better self of Los's emanation, Enitharmon. Urizen could discover and destroy this vision of the fruitful eternal relationship of the contraries and thereby destroy the means by which man must be regenerated. Los, the prophetic spirit, must therefore hide Enitharmon from Urizen, and indeed from the raw energy of Orc as well. This he does:

> . . . Los encircled Enitharmon
> With fires of Prophecy
> From the sight of Urizen & Orc.

Urizen, however, continues to look around his world, but now he sickens at what he sees. It swims with enormities, scraps and similitudes of the human Eternity:

> . . . his world teemd vast enormities
> Frightning; faithless; fawning
> Portions of life; similitudes
> Of a foot, or a hand, or a head
> Or a heart, or an eye, they swam mischevous
> Dread terrors! delighting in blood[.]

He sickens most at the sight of his eternal creations, now become his coporeal sons and daughters, and he begins to see that 'no flesh nor spirit could keep / His iron laws one moment'. For he recognizes that in his world of destructive conflicts and pity 'life liv'd upon death'; that is, the central characteristic of his world is the ontological counterpart of pity, which divides his world and hence makes a single law impossible. Thus, Urizen's world is an absurdity and based on self-destruction—though he does not fully realize it even yet—for not only is it animated by forces which are destructively opposed, but it is in principle a divided existence in which one half of life lives upon the death of the other half.

In the rest of *The Book of Urizen* Blake further shows Urizen's absurdity and impotence by another ironic twist. He shows that it is owing to Urizen's very sorrow at his own failure that he achieves what little success he does achieve. The 'web of religion', which imposes further limits on Urizen's people, causing them in a measure to follow single laws by further destroying their perceptions, is formed from his sorrow at his failure to enforce his laws. After recognizing that 'no flesh nor spirit could keep / His iron laws one moment', he had wandered in sorrow:

> 7. Till a Web dark & Cold, thoughout all
>   The tormented element stretch'd
>   From the sorrows of Urizens soul
>   And the Web is a Female in embrio.
>   None could break the Web, no wings of fire.
>
> 8. So twisted the cords, & so knotted
>   The meshes: twisted like to the human brain
>
> 9. And all calld it, The Net of Religion.

The net is spun like a spider's web and made to fit the human mind exactly, or what is left of it in the fallen world. When the net is imposed on the inhabitants of the cities, their senses shrink further, cutting them off both from a knowledge of Eternity and from a knowledge of what it was that cut them off—from a knowledge of the net itself:

> . . . the shrunken eyes clouded over
> Discernd not the woven hipocrisy
> But the streaky slime in their heavens
> Brought together by narrowing perceptions
> Appeard transparent air; for their eyes
> Grew small like the eyes of a man. . . .

The effect is like that of looking through a window screen and growing unconscious of the meshes. With the final restriction of the senses, the creation of Urizen's world is complete.

The argument given in the Preludium of the *Book of Urizen* announced that the subject was to be religion. Blake has taken the long way round in getting to religion as such, but in doing so he has shown by means of a penetrating irony that the religion of repression is an outgrowth of that great philosophical error, the denial of the contraries and of the dynamism of human life which they constitute.

In a general sense, this idea is essentially the same as that expressed by *The Marriage*. But Blake's conception of the contraries in *The Book of Urizen* has undergone some refinements and a shift of emphasis. Not only has he distinguished oppositions into two kinds, the contraries of Eternity and the negations of this world, but he has shifted from the dialectical significance he had given his doctrine in *The Marriage* to a more purely apocalyptic significance in *The Book of Urizen*. He has cast the two kinds of oppositions into the two worlds of his critical dualism and no longer suggests, as he did in *The Marriage*, that the conflict of the oppositions of this world can lead to the oppositions in Eternity. Now Eternity is to be approached only through the apocalyptic fires of prophecy behind which Los has hidden Enitharmon from the sight of the negations, Urizen and Orc. This shift is evident in the approach to the oppositions of this world employed by Blake in the two works. In *The Marriage* he begins with good and evil and attempts a synthesis of them in the classical manner, by showing that both are but species of necessarily contrary genuses. In *The Book of Urizen*, however, he approaches the oppositions of this world downward, so to speak, from those of the higher world of Eternity, thereby emphasizing their differences, rather than their similarities. Though he does not use the word 'negations' in this book, the distinction between contraries and negations, which marks his abandonment of his initial dialectical scheme, is clearly implied by the structure of the myth itself. And it is this new apocalyptic idea of the contraries which represents Blake's maturer version of his doctrine, and which we shall see further developed in *Milton*.

Urizen is lavishly illuminated; but the remaining books of Blake's 'Bible of Hell', *The Book of Ahania* and *The Book of Los*, which exist in a unique copy each, were engraved in the ordinary way, not in illuminated printing, and were illustrated by colour printing, a method of putting pigments on a flat board and pressing it on to paper. These works fit with *Urizen*, *The Book of Ahania* picking up the narrative where *Urizen* leaves off and *The Book of Los* telling the story of the Fall from Los's point of view and intersecting the narrative of *Urizen*.

Urizen ends with the exodus from Egypt under the leadership of Fuzon, one of Urizen's sons, Blake's analogue to Moses:

> 8. So Fuzon call'd all together
>   The remaining children of Urizen:
>   And they left the pendulous earth:
>   They called it Egypt, & left it.

In *Ahania* Fuzon takes on a Promethean character and with fiery wrath attacks Urizen verbally as a 'Demon of smoke', an

> . . . abstract non-entity
> This cloudy God seated on waters
> Now seen, now obscur'd; King of sorrow[.]

The attack then turns to sexual warfare. He heaves a burning globe at Urizen which tears through his shield forged in wintry mills and castrates him, 'the cold loins of Urizen dividing', as is common in the attacks of mythical sons on their fathers. In sexual anguish, Urizen divides into himself and his emanation Ahania, his 'parted soul'. And in the ambivalent jealousy of his divided self, he puts her away from him, while 'kissing her and weeping over her', and calls her Sin.

Urizen then sets about preparing a black bow with a rock poisoned by a serpent, as a sort of phallic substitute, and shoots it at Fuzon, who thinks Urizen dead and himself god, 'the eldest of things'. The rock kills Fuzon and then becomes 'Mount Sinai in Arabia'. Urizen carries the body to the tree of mystery, which grows like the banyan by forming roots and new trunks from limbs touching the ground until it becomes a grove and a maze, and he nails the body of Fuzon to the tree. Fuzon becomes thereby a version, or perhaps an imitation, of Christ, at least in Christ's corporeal aspect as a dying god of sacrifice, which in *The Four Zoas* will be signalled by his putting on 'Luvah's robes of blood'. Urizen's triumph over Fuzon by this crucifixion can be taken to suggest that Urizenic religion will similarly crucify any one who rebels against it and that Christ himself might be regarded as such a rebel, as Blake said he was in *The Marriage*.

Pestilence flies round the body, and disease spreads. Los, as in *Urizen*, beats on his anvil trying to give shape to the body, now reduced to bones. After forty years of pestilence, and of the hardening of Urizen's children's skulls, echoing the forty years' wandering of the children of Israel, Asia arises as a solid continent, as Fuzon groans on the tree.

The rest of this work consists of Ahania's lament for her lost Urizen before his fall, before jealousy:

9. When he gave my happy soul
   To the sons of eternal joy:
   When he took the daughters of life.
   Into my chambers of love[.]

Then Urizen, 'with a lap full of seed' which he no longer has, was productive and creative:

   With thy hand full of generous fire
   Walked forth from the clouds of morning
   On the virgins of springing joy,
   On the human soul to cast
   The seed of eternal science.

But now he has become 'self-destroying'.

The Book of Los can be inserted into the middle of *Urizen* as an alternate version of Los's labours to give form to the hurtling chaos begun by Urizen and form to Urizen himself as having the body of fallen man. The narrative is related by an ancient 'aged Mother' who remembers the 'Times remote' before the fall:

   When Love & Joy were adoration:
   And none impure were deem'd.

> Not Eyeless Covet
> Nor Thin-lip'd Envy
> Nor Bristled Wrath
> Nor Curled Wantonness[.]

Covet, Envy, Wrath, and Wantonness were fulfilled, and even they were not impure. So they changed their natures. But suddenly the narrative shifts to a view of Los, bound in a chain, compelled to watch Urizen's shadow being created in his abstract, self-closed system, the solid without fluctuation created in *Urizen*.

Los succumbs to his prophetic wrath and cracks the whole creation, which then begins to hurtle and fall, and Los falls with it. Blake may be borrowing from Lucretius's stream of atoms which must swerve from their parallel paths for creation to occur, for Los does the same thing:

> 6. The Immortal revolving; indignant
>   First in wrath threw his limbs, like the babe
>   New born into our world: wrath subsided
>   And contemplative thoughts first arose
>   Then aloft his head rear'd in the Abyss
>   And his downward-borne fall chang'd oblique[.]

The rest of the book is then spent in describing Los's labours in creating the body of Urizen. The version of this process in *Urizen* was evidently the one Blake liked best, because he brings it into *The Four Zoas*, which he was shortly to begin or might already have begun in its original form of *Vala*.

The story of the Fall as it is told in the Lambeth prophecies just discussed will be greatly elaborated and enlarged upon in *The Four Zoas*. And in that work Blake will add to the story of man's Fall his regeneration in a stupendous apocalypse. The structure of Blake's myth will continue to have points of contact with the Bible throughout, bit it will not be formulated quite so explicitly as a 'Bible of Hell', as it is in the Lambeth prophecies which tell the story of the Fall. These prophecies, delivered as books formally follow the structure of the Bible, with some influences from the epic of a bard, or, in *The Book of Los*, an aged mother. The later prophecies will develop in new and unusual forms.

7 | *The Four Zoas*

The Four Zoas, which Northrop Frye has called 'the greatest abortive masterpiece in English literature',[1] presents a host of special critical difficulties because it remained a work in progress that began with one poem, called *Vala*, and continued as another one which absorbed the first. It was never engraved. The MS is a mass of additions, deletions, and revisions that were made over many years; and, while editors have been able to come to a reasonable agreement as to what order its parts can be assembled in to form a workable reading text, we do not have a version of it that can be confidently taken as representing Blake's final intentions, which we would have had only if he had engraved it.[2] But in whatever form it is read, it remains, despite gaps in internal detailed coherence, the product of an all-but incredible imaginative energy.

The title given originally on the first sheet was: VALA / OR / The Death and / Judgement / of the / Ancient Man / A DREAM / of Nine Nights / by William Blake 1797. But later the title on this sheet was changed to *The Four Zoas / The Torments of Love and Jealousy in / The Death and Judgement / of Albion the / Ancient Man*. Vala was removed from the title and so was the description of the poem as a dream of nine nights.

In the original poem of *Vala*, plausibly reconstructed by H. M. Margoliouth after painstaking scrutiny of the MS, Vala was to have a central role, but she diminishes in importance as the poem develops.[3] Vala is the feminine counterpart of Luvah, who falls to be Orc; and, though none of Blake's mythological characters should be thought of as personifications of abstractions, it can be said that she represents something like the nature which comes between man and his mental or imaginative powers. Her effect is not wholly dissimilar to that of nature as a 'homely nurse' in

Wordsworth's Immortality Ode in separating man from his primordial vision, or Coleridge's 'film of familiarity and selfish solicitude' in consequence of which 'we have eyes, yet see not, ears that hear not, and hearts that neither feel nor understand'.[4]

Blake had got far enough with this poem to have made a fair copy of much of it in a careful hand and had sketched on to his MS pages designs, presumably for engraving. But somewhere in the process he expanded his conception enormously in a way that brought together many fragments of the myth that had appeared in the prophecies of the earlier 1790s. The central part of this new conception involved making three of his earlier characters, Urizen, Los, and Orc, fallen versions of essential constituents of Man, called Albion, and adding a fourth, Tharmas. In their unfallen condition they are: Urizen, Urthona, Luvah, and Tharmas, respectively. They become the 'zoas' whose four natures in harmony symbolize total unfallen man. Blake calls them zoas, forming the word, as Frye suggests by adding an English plural to a Greek root meaning animal or living creature, adapting from Ezekiel and other sources the allegorical symbol for the divine state of the chariot drawn by animals.[5] Blake even uses the phrase 'vehicular form' for the body as the 'form of the soul's energy', and thus with marvellous directness fashions his composite symbol of Man (whose local habitation he prefers to place in England as Albion) and his four natures. Again with a caveat against too literal allegorization, the zoas have associations as follows: Urizen, the abstract scientific intellect and the head; Luvah, passion and generative love and the loins, whom the Fall changed into Orc; Urthona, work in the service of vision, and the feet, whom the Fall changes into Los; and finally Tharmas, the least developed of the zoas, as something like a principle of integration, or perhaps power, and the breast.

The associations do not stop there. Blake, who had one of the most schematic imaginations in literature, buttressed by an idea of correspondences, sees additional associations with the zoas. A long list of these is suggested by Frye, but we might note a few of the most important ones, using some of Frye's categories:[6]

Eternal name	Luvah	Urizen	Tharmas	Urthona
Time name	Orc	Satan	Covering Cherub	Los
Emanation	Vala	Ahania	Enion	Enitharmon
Quality	Love	Wisdom	Power	Fancy
Sense	Nose	Eye	Tongue	Ear

Body part	Loins	Head	Heart	Legs
Element	Fire	Air	Water	Earth
Compass point	East	South	West	North

Some of the imagery of *The Four Zoas* may seem more mysterious than it really is if we are unaware of these associations.

We have encountered emanations before, in Ahania as the emanation of Urizen and Enitharmon as the emanation of Los. But now Blake matches each of the zoas with a female counterpart, who is divided from the zoa in the Fall, and adds Vala as the emanation of Luvah (Orc) and Enion as that of Tharmas. In Eternity the sexes were not divided. The union of the sexes, however, was not an hermaphroditic one but an androgynous one, a union of creative contraries rather than merely one individual with both sexes. The division into fallen sexuality tends to create the war of the sexes in which the contrary aspects of the androgyne, being split off from one another, no longer always see their common ground as contraries and behave like negations, denying each other while still being attracted, as Urizen in *Ahania* rejected Ahania as sin while kissing her and weeping over her. Some of the emanations do not try to gain female dominion over their male counterparts but merely lament their lost union, as Enion does of Tharmas for almost the whole of *The Four Zoas*. And there is nothing inherently evil about the emanation, though she may behave perversely in consciousness of her fallen sexuality, as a coy mistress using her attractiveness to gain power. Ideally, in Eternity—and potentially on earth—the emanation, as the word implies, is something like a projection of an ideal in an objective form, an embodiment of love. Enitharmon, who in *Europe* was a malevolent Queen of Heaven, becomes in *The Four Zoas* an helpmeet for Los, after a period as a fallen female tormenting him: and they work together building Golgonooza, the city of art, preparing for the advent of Jerusalem, the city of God.

Albion, or 'Man', the total form of humanity of whom the zoas are aspects, also has an emanation, who is Jerusalem, symbolically his female part but also the city of God to which Man will return at the apocalypse. Put very simply, the great task of Los and his emanation Enitharmon will be to bring Man and his emanation Jerusalem back together again. Man became separated from his emanation in a crucial event that is obscurely reported by several witnesses in *The Four Zoas* as recollection of something which occurred on a 'dread day'. Somehow Man was seduced by Vala, and the eternal functions of Urizen and Luvah were displaced, producing a chaotic chain reaction occurring in a moment but with consequences through all of human history.

The original title of the poem contained the words 'A Dream of Nine Nights', but this was deleted. *The Four Zoas*, no less than *Vala*, remains a dream of Albion the Ancient Man. The nine nights into which it is arranged reflect the structure of Edward Young's *Night Thoughts*, a meditative poem on mortality usually associated with the 'graveyard school' of English poetry. Blake made over five hundred water-colour designs for the poem. Some of *The Four Zoas* is written in the blocked off areas of the folio proof sheets left for letterpress printing of the text of Young's poem amidst the surrounding designs, and most of the rest of it is written on the backs of the sheets.

But Young's poem is a meditation, and most of Blake's is a dream of the giant Albion, who begins to stir at the beginning of night eight and sneezes, becoming fully awake in the astonishing *tour de force* of night nine of the apocalypse. The dream structure of this work accounts for much of its difficulty. Blake had used the dream of Enitharmon in *Europe* as a means of organizing a visionary account of 1800 years of human history around certain controlling patterns of imagery, and of course all the prophecies thus far put visions into motion in mythical narrative. But his structural models for these works were—if only as ghostly paradigms of models— the epic and the biblical narrative. In *The Four Zoas* he can be freer. The work proceeds not so much by narration as by dramatic scenes, speeches, songs, and choruses. In fact it is more like a fantastic opera than anything else. And there are numerous flash-backs told in speeches that stop the action and go back to memories of the old times, much as might be done in arias. Blake's frequent specification of instrumentation suggests that he heard incidental music for it; and rather unusual instrumentation it is. Blake uses trumpets and horns a good deal, and he also likes flutes and strings for the softer parts, but he seems especially fond of small drums and cymbals for rhythmic accent. In the ninth night even the 'tygers from the forests & the lions from the sandy deserts . . . sieze the instruments of harmony' (E 378; K 365).[7] There are numerous dances, the most notable being Los's convulsive St. Vitus dance, 'Infected Mad', at the beginning of night five, while Enitharmon is soothed on her couch by the music of 'the soft pipe the flute the viol organ harp & cymbal' (E 332; K 306).

Another structural feature of *The Four Zoas*, and one which derives most directly from dream, is the use of a recurrent image in a vision of Jesus descending in Luvah's 'robes of blood'. This image, which is modulated in various ways, reappears at crucial points and expresses the idea that Jesus puts on mortality in becoming, like Luvah, a dying god of the generative world redeeming man by forgiving the sin He is made to suffer in the crucifixion. Jesus also appears with a 'Council of God', which is a development in a more explicitly Christian context of the society of Eternals from the *Book of Urizen*. But the image-cluster of Jesus in Luvah's robes that simply reappears as a vision becomes one of the polar controlling images of the work. It is brought in as being opposed to the events of the obscure dread day when the Fall began and Albion went to sleep. The passage of Jesus into bloody mortality is reversed in the bloody vintage of the apocalypse when Man puts off mortality in the 'harvest and vintage of nations'.

More than the prophecies written up to that time, *The Four Zoas* resists allegorization. An attempt to read it, or understand it, by conceptual translation results in frustration. For the actors in this cosmic drama are by no means personified abstractions who can be easily labelled by their attributes. They carry with them a host of very carefully worked out associations, including, in addition to the ones noted briefly earlier, some political associations. Luvah, for instance, as Erdman has shown, can be identified with France at the level of political allegory, and Urizen with England; and at some points in the action, the political allegory becomes paramount. But Blake's characters must be taken seriously as real personages in a strange phantasmagoric drama if one is to enter into this work in a way that leads to understanding of the kind that Blake wanted to communicate, through his 'allegory addressed to the intellectual powers'. One must, that is, first enter the work as one would any other imaginative work by an appropriate suspension of disbelief despite its strangeness and simply accept what happens as actually happening even when it is altogether fantastic. Then, later, one can pursue the implications of some of these marvellous events. *The Four Zoas* is one of the richest and most intellectually demanding of Blake's prophecies; but at the same time, because of its dramatic character and its sheer poetry, it is one of the most accessible.

If space permitted an extended commentary on this poem, some of the new conceptions that Blake introduces here, or some older ones that become important, could be discussed as they came up. But this is clearly impossible in a brief introductory survey of Blake's work. So instead, I shall attempt to sketch a few aspects of the cosmic stage on which this drama is played and describe a few functional elements, in the hope that they will be more readily recognizable when encountered in the poem itself. My indebtedness to the brilliant account of *The Four Zoas* by Northrop Frye in *Fearful Symmetry* (1947), from which modern Blake criticism really derives, is only too evident, and I strongly recommend any reader to consult it—after he has grappled with the primary text. My purpose here is merely to provide an introduction to the text so that deeper study may follow.

Blake's organizing of his myth in *The Four Zoas* makes explicit several ideas that were implicit but perhaps incompletely formulated in earlier work, and which it will be essential to have clearly in mind not only for this work but for the last two great epics, *Milton* and *Jerusalem*. Most important of these is the structure of his cosmos, which is divided into four levels: Eden or Eternity, Beulah, Generation, and Ulro. Earlier we noted four levels of vision, and these have a correspondence with these levels of being. Fourfold vision yields a perception that reveals all being as one, or as total and 'organized', characteristically as One Man, Jesus; threefold vision involves the perceiver in a transformation analogous to the transformation of the eye of a lover in beholding his or her beloved, or possibly a loving parent looking at a child; twofold vision is a perception of ordinary external reality but under the aspect of the other superior levels of vision and hence sees all being in a way that connects one part with any other part, as in the metaphorical perception that sees in the similarities of things connections between those things; and, finally, single vision is merely passive physical perception that consists of nothing but sense data, especially under the aspect of a conception of reality that excludes everything but material existence, a conception Blake calls 'single vision or Newton's sleep'.

Eden might be identified with heaven had not orthodox religion appropriated that region as its special domain for its angels and starry hosts, and conceived it as existing somehow in space, 'up there', an abode for a Nobodaddy or a fallen Urizen. So Blake calls it Eden, partly to suggest that it is the primordial state from which man fell and partly to suggest that it is attainable not by going to some other place physically but by changing man's vision of himself and of his relation to God, on earth. In the action of the prophecies, Eden, or Eternity, almost has to be represented in the spatial categories of the fallen world, as being up rather than down; but whenever he can Blake turns space inside out and makes imaginative space inside, as he did in the Printing House in Hell in *The Marriage*. Eden, as a place or a habitation, is out of space; and Eternity, of course, as the root meaning of the word suggests, is out of time.

Below Eden or Eternity, at the threefold level, is the state of Beulah, a word which comes from Isaiah and means married. As threefold vision invests perception with love and delight that springs from love, Beulah is a state of love and enjoyment that is, under the aspect of Eden, a softer state than Eden. In the intense creativity of Eden, the contraries engage in vigorous but productive 'mental war', but in Beulah the opposition of the contraries is suspended. It is a sort of rest camp for the mental warriors. Beulah, however, is a 'sexual' state as Blake's numerological designation of it as threefold indicates. And while it is a necessary state for man in a life that includes the intense mental conflict of Eden, it can also be perverted by being cut off from Eden and the fourfold scheme of being. Properly considered, it is, as Frye says, 'a lower paradise'. But if this cool paradise is confused with Eden, as representing the ultimate in human existence, a perversion results which can turn out to be destructive. This is essentially what happens in the later lyric, 'The Crystal Cabinet', in which the speaker strives to grasp the 'inmost form' in a threefold sexual experience and finds himself suddenly in a wasteland. Something similar happens in Keats's 'La Belle Dame Sans Merci'.

Beulah, therefore, while not itself creative, provides a necessary condition for recreation and rest from creative activity. But it can also be delusive and hence destructive. Its character depends on whether it is orientated toward Eden as the ultimate paradise or toward the state below it, Generation—without the consciousness that Beulah derives its meaning from Eden and not, as a kind of sublimated sexuality, from Generation. Without the redeeming fourfold vision of Eden, Beulah as a threefold state becomes merely sexual and hence malevolent. And man is susceptible in Beulah: the

Fall in *The Four Zoas* occurs in Beulah, when Vala seduces Albion, and Luvah and Urizen exchange functions. The numbers four and three have special numerological significance, both as integers and as raised by powers. The number four, or any power of it, indicates something consistent with Eden. Three, or threefold, can have a benign connotation if it is clearly associated with the fourfold scheme, as Beulah can be; but otherwise, and most usually, it has a malevolent association. Cubing three yields twenty-seven in the twenty-seven churches from Adam to Luther and represents a systemization of threefoldness. Multiplying three by four yields twelve, which has associations with the Zodiac and clock time and signals some kind of perversion of vision, as in the reduction of the divisions of the Sons of Albion from sixteen divisions (four squared) to twelve, in *Jerusalem* (E 227; K 715).

Below Beulah is Generation, the ordinary world we live in, the world of nature. Within the fourfold scheme, nature, as a twofold state, is redeemed by the divine imagination and hence is benign. Ideally it is where man eats and sleeps and works with a consciousness that his life derives its meaning from the informing vision of the states above it. Blake himself gives conflicting testimony on his attitude toward the world of nature, often making extreme statements even denying its existence, but at other times explaining (as he did to the unspiritual clergyman, Dr Trusler) that everything he paints he sees in this world, and that this world is one of joy, and calling this world 'Holy generation, image of regeneration'.[8] But when he denies the external world, what he usually means is that he denies it as the criterion of reality, or as the only reality. External nature does exist; but for human life it is barren without the redeeming vision of the divine imagination. In the world properly perceived, 'Everything that lives is holy'.[9]

Generation, like Beulah, is susceptible to perversion and in the same way. If one cuts Generation off from the redeeming vision and takes it to be the only reality there is, it becomes thereby tyrannical. Blake embraces the idea that life is cyclic, and he often represents Eternity in images of wheels. The life cycle in Eternity is a benign one in which winter is a period of rest when 'females sleep' and then arise in joy with songs. This is the natural cycle as redeemed by vision, and its emphasis is on the renewal of life. But in nature without vision, the cycle has no meaning beyond mere repetition. As Peter F. Fisher said in *The Valley of Vision* (Toronto

1961), 'the teleology of nature is death': the natural cycle as such emphasizes not renewal but death. Without the informing divine vision, nature becomes spiritually barren and merely exists. It is then fallen, and the life lived in it is a fallen existence.

From fallen Generation it is only a step to the next state below it, Ulro, or a sort of hell, which represents a further stage in the Fall. Ulro is not only at the bottom of the levels of being but it is not redeemable as Generation is. Eden gives meaning to all the four levels and is a fourfold state. Beulah is itself a state and is related to those above and below it, and hence is a threefold state. Generation is a state in itself at the second degree and is also connected, by wrong-headed metaphysics, to Ulro and hence is a two-fold state. But Ulro is at the bottom and hence single. Ulro represents the results of a metaphysical perversion of Generation into an abstraction of it as mere corporeal reality. It is a state with no creative potential at all because it is a dead abstraction. Only destruction of life occurs in its arid waste of rocks and sand. While it cannot be redeemed by vision, it exists, if only as a potentiality, and it must be known. It is the state of Satan, and 'Satan must be new created continually moment by moment'.[10] Ulro should be emptied of inhabitants, but Ulro itself must remain and be understood in order to be avoided.

Blake borrows from St Paul, Ephesians vi, 12, an epigraph which he quotes in Greek and which reads in the King James version:

For we wrestle not against flesh and blood, but against principalities, against powers, against the rulers of the darkness of this world, against spiritual wickedness in high places. (E 296; K 263)

This passage comes from Paul's urging of the Ephesians to put on the 'whole armour of God', having loins girt with truth, the breast plate of righteousness, the feet shod with 'the preparation of the gospel of peace', and the helmet of salvation. However Paul intended this, Blake read it to mean that the struggle of spirit would not be with flesh but with institutionalized oppression and entrenched spiritual perversion; and he finds in Paul's metaphor of the armour of God another biblical version of the four zoas, in addition to his citations to John xvii and John i. He does not mention Isaiah i, 5ff and Revelation iv, 6, which are clearly relevant.

It is most unfortunate that at the very beginning of the first night the text is such a mess of deletions and revisions that any transcription fails to make good sense, and a reader trying to get into this work is apt to give up on the opening page. Blake was going to have the poem be the 'Song of the Aged Mother', Eno, who speaks *The Song of Los*, but after struggling with the opening lines he evidently decided to let the muse be a 'Daughter of Beulah'. From these opening lines we can get the doctrine of the 'Four Mighty Ones . . . in every Man', the four zoas, that there will be a 'day of Intellectual Battle' in the apocalypse in Night IX, and that Los will be a principal figure in the narrative because he is singled out for particular attention:

> Los was the fourth immortal starry one, & in the Earth
> Of a bright Universe Empery attended day & night
> Days & nights of revolving joy, Urthona was his name
> In Eden; in the Auricular Nerves of Human life
> Which is the Earth of Eden, he his Emanations propagated
> Fairies of Albion afterwards Gods of the Heathen,
> Daughter of Beulah Sing
> His fall into Division & his Resurrection to Unity[.]   (E 297; K 264)

The larger matter of this lengthy song, of course, is the Fall of Albion into division and his resurrection, and Los in this division is but one of the four mighty ones. But as the prophetic spirit, he is the father of all mythology—as Urthona—and hence embodies man's imagination. In associating him with earth and the feet that walk on earth, as well as making him into a smith, Blake is suggesting that imagination should own the earth and cannot be thought of apart from work.

The story could begin with any of the zoas because they are so closely interconnected. Blake begins 'with Tharmas Parent power, darkning in the West', and he plunges swiftly *in medias res*, after the first steps in the Fall, with a dramatic scene between Tharmas and his emanation, Enion. Jealousy has set everything into emotional chaos, and Tharmas tries to explain himself to a jealous and analytical Enion, who examines 'every little fibre of [his] soul'. All existence is in the primal chaos out of which God in Genesis made the creation, and it is watery, as befits Tharmas. We do not learn the real beginning of the story until later, from a variety of witnesses among the emanations, who give slightly different versions of it, as their memories fade or are distorted in their fallen state. The first of these recollections occurs in the first night in Enitharmon's 'Song

f Death', on p. 10 of the MS, and it will serve to give us the
ssentials of the event:

> The Fallen Man takes his repose: Urizen sleeps in the porch
> Luvah and Vala woke & flew up from the Human Heart
> Into the Brain; from thence upon the pillow Vala slumber'd.
> And Luvah siez'd the Horses of Light, & rose into the Chariot of
>   Day
> Sweet laughter siezd me in my sleep! silent & close I laughd
> For in the visions of Vala I walked with the mighty Fallen One
> I heard his voice among the branches, & among sweet flowers.
>   (E 301; K 271)

This passage is richly complex and an attempt at a full explication
f it would occupy us for much more space than is available. But
. brief gloss is possible and might be helpful. The Fall of Albion
tarts in Beulah, the 'sexual' state of repose. As we noted earlier,
3eulah is an state intermediate between Eden and Generation and
as connections with both. The unfallen Urizen, as ideal intellectual
ower that gives form and order to existence, and in Eden is, or
as control of, the sun that moves in terrific cycles, is asleep in the
orch. But Luvah and Vala, who are associated with the generative
ycle, wake, and fly up from the loins—in the geography of Albion's
ody—through the heart up into the brain. In other words, they
eave their proper generative region, traverse that of Tharmas and
bsorb his power, and finally move to Urizen's region in the brain.
To translate this allegorically: to attain efficiency, the process of
generative power usurps intellectual power, and the cyclical
unctions of the generative world impose themselves on the re-
urrent order of Eden as, in a sense, administered by Urizen; so
he cyclical process of life will now become a cyclical process of
death under the influence of the nature god Luvah, who is a dying
god. Or, to put it another way, the idea of sexuality as something
eparable from the totality of human life enters the mind of the
leeping Albion, and this implies the idea of a separate Female Will,
mbodied by Vala, who 'thence upon the pillow . . . slumber'd' as
is mistress in both senses of that word.

The ideal order of Eden has been taken over by the repressive
ycle of nature, which is the Female Will in action. In this first
ight of *The Four Zoas*, Blake takes considerable pains—for him—
o explain certain theoretical concepts that operate in his myth, and
ne of these is the benign kind of cyclicity in Eden:

> In Eden Females sleep the winter in soft silken veils
> Woven by their own hands to hide them in the darksom grave
> But Males immortal live renewd by female deaths. in soft
> Delight they die & they revive in spring with music & songs[.]
> (E 298; K 266)

Though Blake is open to the charge of being a male chauvinist, he
is attempting to portray here the ideal sexual cycle, indentifying the
female body, because of its sexually cyclical rhythms, with the
rhythms of nature. And he is showing a benign reconciliation of
Innocence and Experience. The cycle is one which emphasizes
regeneration, and the period before regeneration, though called
death, is merely a sleep or a fallow period of rest. The cycle of
nature also includes a renewal, but it follows a 'nether course' that
is orientated to death. In the second night Blake gives one description of it:

> . . . the stars of heaven created like a golden chain
>
> . . .
>
> . . . travelling along even to its destind end
> Then falling down. a terrible space recovring in winter dire
> Its wasted strength. it back returns upon a nether course
> Till fired with ardour fresh recruited in its humble season
> It rises up on high all summer till its wearied course
> Turns into autumn.   (E 315; K 287)

From autumn emerges the monster Winter, from *Poetical Sketches*
   When Luvah usurps Urizen's function as presiding over the
cyclical process of Eden, the benign recurrence that had redeemed
the cycle of nature is subverted, and life now takes on only the
destructive cyclicity of nature and of human life in the fallen world
This involves that continuing conflict between Urizen and Luvah
who later becomes Orc, which Northrop Frye has taught us to call
the 'Orc cycle'.
   Blake wants to make the distinction between Eternal and fallen
cyclicity clear at the end of Night I:

> Terrific ragd the Eternal Wheels of intellect terrific ragd
> The living creatures of the wheels in the Wars of Eternal life
> But perverse rolld the wheels of Urizen & Luvah back reversd
> Downwards & outwards consuming in the wars of Eternal Death[.]
> (E 309; K 280)

Before the Fall, cyclical motion was freewheeling and creative, but after it the wheels become gears that involve and compel each other. The image of gears is apt, for Urizen and Orc, though they move in opposite directions, are part of a common process. In Luvah's taking over the sun, the sun is debased into a flaming orb that governs the deathful cycle of the seasons in generation; and for Urizen, lost in abstraction, it becomes thereafter the symbol of a system that moves not as a terrifically raging wheel of intellect but with abstract 'mathematic motion' (E 315; K 287).

Albion's mental projection of a separate Female as cryptically described in Enitharmon's 'Song of Death' is paralleled later on, in Night III, by his similar projection of the Other to worship, forgetting that 'all deities reside in the human breast'. Projection of an external deity is the formulation of the idea of 'the holy' in a way that makes worship a function of the self-debasement of the worshipper:

> O I am nothing when I enter into judgment with thee
> If thou withdraw thy breath I die & vanish into Hades[.]
> (E 321; K 293)

In other words, Albion is denying his own humanity and thus his own existence, and hence moving toward the state that Blake calls 'eternal death', beyond the limits of redemption. This projection of the idea of the holy is rather like the projection of the idea of the Female, Vala, because it confers power on something external and diminishes humanity.

I apologize for this long digression to events preceding the opening of *The Four Zoas*, but knowing the beginning of the story, I think, helps make the narrative easier to follow. To return, then, to the narrative. After Tharmas tries to explain himself to Enion and complains of her being analytical, Blake introduces a brief theoretical passage on Edenic cyclicity, which we noted above. In her fallen state, Enion said 'I die', and Tharmas stretched out his hand in sorrow turning round the circle of destiny and saying, 'Return O Wanderer when the Day of Clouds is oer' (E 298; K 266). Enion had been weaving a tabernacle for Jerusalem but now begins to weave the 'Spectre' of Tharmas. In the meantime, the circle of destiny—the tyrannical chain of fallen cause and effect —is complete. At this point, Blake introduces another short theoretical passage describing Beulah, as a 'mild & pleasant rest', a 'Soft

Moony Universe feminine lovely', which is created by Jesus to form providential spaces to prevent men from falling to eternal death. The daughters of Beulah create a space for the circle of destiny 'and namd the Space Ulro & brooded over it in care & love' (E 299; K 267).

Blake also lets them give a bit more theory, this time on the spectre:

> They said The Spectre is in every man insane & most
> Deformd Thro the three heavens descending in fury & fire
> We meet it with our Songs & loving blandishments & give
> To it a form of vegetation But this Spectre of Tharmas
> Is Eternal Death What shall we do O God pity & help
> So spoke they & closd the Gate of the Tongue in trembling fear[.]
> (E 299; K 267)

The spectre in Blake is the workaday self that meets the ordinary obligations of the individual. In a harmonious individual, one who reflects consciousness of an organized identity consistent with humanity, the spectre works for the individual, as later on the ambiguous Spectre of Urthona will work for Los in building Golgonooza. But the spectre in and of itself has a tendency to become brutish, 'insane and most Deformd', unless it is assimilated to the order of fourfold vision by being given spatial form by Beulah. The Spectre of Tharmas, however, has been cut off from Tharmas and takes on a will of its own. There is no redeeming it in the spatial forms of Generation. Accordingly, the daughters of Beulah, frightened by this divided embodiment of unregenerable 'eternal death', close the gate to Paradise associated with Tharmas, the gate of the tongue—which might be allegorically glossed as closing off the possibility of regeneration through ordinary discourse. The Fall has moved a stage farther.

The Spectre becomes an incarnate will, full of pride. He has a sexual union with the fallen Enion, and from it are born Los and Enitharmon as two sullen infants. These two figure prominently in the shorter prophecies without explanation as to who they are or how they got there; but now Blake not only provides a means for getting them on to his stage but follows their development, because Los has become more clearly defined as the agent of regeneration whose 'fall into division' is an important part of the story.

Los and Enitharmon as infants sulk upon Enion's breast, as does the infant of Experience in 'Infant Sorrow', and Enion begins to age as they take away her youth in the cycles of fallen nature, in an anticipation of the deathful cycles of 'The Mental Traveller'. They wander away from her, and Enion, like a Demeter, searches for them. But they scorn her, causing pangs of maternal love if only of a spectrous kind, which goes out to them. In the process, they draw out all her spectrous life, which had made possible her union with the prideful Spectre of Tharmas, and she becomes a mourning earth mother whose lament at the end of Night II is one of the most concrete and poignant passages in the poem, an extended Song of Experience from the point of view of the earth.

Then time and space are created by a daughter of Beulah, under the influence of the 'Hand Divine' of Jesus, whose influence attends all events in the narrative but whose presence is not yet known. Los and Enitharmon, older now, exercise the contrarious emotions of the fallen world in time and space:

> Alternate Love & Hate his breast; hers Scorn & Jealousy
> In embryon passions. they kiss'd not nor embrac'd for shame &
> fear[.]   (E 301; K 240)

And Enitharmon sings her 'Song of Death', already noticed.

Los hits her and rejects the burden of her song of female dominion seeing the relationship between Albion and Vala differently, and prophetically seeing that Luvah will become a dying god and so the corporeal war that will ensue:

> . . . Beware the punishment
> I see, invisible descend into the Gardens of Vala
> Luvah walking on the winds, I see the invisible knife
> I see the shower of blood: I see the swords & spears of futurity[.]
> (E 302; K 272)

Enitharmon, furious at this, calls upon Urizen in his aspect as 'Father of Jealousy', as Blake earlier had called the god of the female will. Urizen now has a worshipper, and by virtue of that fact descends to proclaim himself a god indeed: 'Now I am God from Eternity to Eternity' (E 302; K 273). He commands Los to worship him, scorning him as a 'visionary of Jesus the soft delusion of Eternity' and flatly asserting that 'The Spectre is the Man the rest is only delusion & fancy' (E 303; K 273). Los repents his striking Enitharmon and feels love for her.

At this point we are given an image of Luvah and Vala in the sky made bloody by Urizen assembling his starry hosts in the battles of the 'swords & spears of futurity' that Los foresaw. And we are also given another image, the thematic one of Jesus in Luvah's robes of blood that will recur and be modulated throughout the poem:

> Eternity appeard above them as One Man infolded
> In Luvah[s] robes of blood & bearing all his afflictions[.]
>   (E 303; K 274)

Rather than digress here to comment on this complex image, I shall defer that for the moment and simply remark that this vision, which appears at crucial points somewhat like a pictorial projection which the reader must see in his mind's eye, keeps Jesus present in the events as a presiding presence and also, of course, anticipates the incarnation and crucifixion of Jesus as the last 'eye of God' before the apocalypse.

After the first appearance of this image, Los and Enitharmon marry in 'discontent & scorn', as a nuptial song is sung with resounding musical accompaniment from 'thunderous Organs' and 'doubling Voices & loud Horns'. The song is sung by Urizen's chorus of the 'thousand thousand' spirits. It is a strange nuptial indeed, full of echoes of war and ending with an anticipation of the birth of Orc—or the change of Luvah into Orc—'Bursting forth from the loins of Enitharmon' (E 305; K 276). Erdman reads this song at the political level as possibly celebrating the 'British defeat of Napoleon in the Mediterranean, possibly conflating the Battle of the Nile (August 1798) and the Siege of Acre (March-May 1799), the first British victory on land.'[11] The scene ends with a lament of Enion, 'blind & age-bent', on the condition of man as it is symbolized in the creatures of nature: Why do the lion and wolf still 'roam abroad'?

Man, or Albion, is then laid to rest by the Saviour on the Rock of Ages, and a 'Council of God' meet in Eternity 'As One Man', Jesus. Four messengers from Beulah report that Albion is sick and Luvah and Urizen 'contend in war around the holy tent' (E 306; K 277). The argument between Urizen and Luvah that ensues makes almost no real sense in the narrative as we have it without reference to political allegory, which Erdman has supplied in detail. Essentially it involves territorial division between Urizen as England and Luvah as France: 'Britain wants a secure hold on the

Netherlands but will recognize Napoleon's conquest of Italy and will even give up most of the captured South Sea Islands', but 'the new France, boastful of the superiority of its "hosts", scorns negotiation'.[12] Thus Urizen proposes 'deep in the North I place my lot / Thou in the South listen attentive', and Luvah replies, 'Dictate to thy Equals. am not I / The Prince of all the hosts of Men nor Equal know in Heaven', Urizen again burns in his tent and discord begins, as Los, who was going to beat his metals into spades and coulters for ploughs, sees his sons leave for the conflict that now resumes.

As the first Night ends, Tharmas hides Enion, Albion is separated from Beulah, Jerusalem his emanation 'is become a ruin / Her little ones are slain on the top of every street', and messengers come from Beulah saying that the oppressors of Jerusalem must be destroyed (E 308; K 279). The Divine Family closes off the Messengers and elects the 'Seven Eyes of God & the Seven lamps of the Almighty', thereby giving form to man's religious history. The seven, identified later, are: Lucifer, Moloch, Elohim, Shaddai, Pachad, Jehovah, and finally Jesus, representing the forms of divinity. After the seventh, Jesus, will come the apocalypse.

The last image of the first Night is that of the 'Eternal Wheels of intellect' as contrasted with the interlocking gears of Urizen and Luvah 'in the wars of Eternal Death'.

In commenting even at this length on the first Night, I have merely skimmed the surface. What I have tried to do is to supply enough introductory information to make reading the first Night easier in the hope that reading the other Nights could follow from that. I should now like to attempt a very brief schematic summary of the rest of the poem, and finally comment a little on Blake's symbolic method, using for illustration the symbol cluster of Jesus wrapped in Luvah's robes of blood.

In Night II, Albion, aware of the ruin that has come about, charges Urizen with the task of building a world. Urizen, 'the great Work master', directs the building of the 'mundane shell', the world under the containing sky, Blake's adaptation of the Orphic egg. In the process, Luvah is 'cast into the Furnaces', which is to say given a body, and from the furnaces he laments in a kind of madness, 'Reasoning from the loins in the unreal forms of Ulros night'. But the building goes on to include a temple of religion in which Urizen's emanation is housed gazing at a false light. Again we are given the presiding vision of the Saviour in Luvah's robes of blood:

> On clouds the Sons of Urizen beheld Heaven walled round
> They weighd & orderd all & Urizen comforted saw
> The wondrous work flow forth like visible out of the invisible
> For the Divine Lamb Even Jesus who is the Divine Vision
> Permitted all lest Man should fall into Eternal Death
> For when Luvah sunk down himself put on the robes of blood
> Lest the state calld Luvah should vease. & the Divine Vision
> Walked in robes of blood till he who slept should awake[.]
>   (E 315; K 287)

Man's passional nature is in danger of being utterly destroyed in the process of giving mathematical form to existence, and Jesus must take on the form of Luvah's passional and generative life to preserve its existence under the aspect of Eternity, for Luvah will shortly be transformed into his Orc aspect. All this time Los and Enitharmon delight in the brave new world, and Enitharmon sings another song of female dominion, with the burden, 'The joy of woman is the Death of her most beloved' (E 317; K 289). The Night ends with another lament from Enion, already noted.

The third Night begins with an echo of Satan in *Paradise Lost* Book II, as Urizen sits exalted on his starry throne. Ahania counsels him to be content with his lot, but Urizen is troubled because he knows of the impending birth of Orc. Ahania then tells him of her vision, in which Albion projects the idea of holiness and of the Other whose worship compels him to deny his own existence. Urizen is angered and asks, 'Am I not God . . . Who is Equal to me[?]' (E 322; K 294) and casts Ahania out by flinging her by the hair. At this 'The Bounds of Destiny crashd direful & the swelling Sea / Burst from its bonds in whirlpools fierce roaring with Human voice' (E 322; K 295). This is Noah's flood, as a deluge probably derived by Blake from Sir Thomas Burnet's *Sacred Theory of the Earth*, in which the deluge occurred by cracking the shell of the earth as the mundane egg to release the waters beneath.[13] All is chaos again, and Tharmas, whose element is water, is once more dominant, but in sorrow; and again Enion appears to lament her loss of Tharmas.

After the deluge, at the beginning of Night IV, Tharmas, now in the ascendancy, wants to die but cannot. He calls on Los to rebuild the ruined universe; but Los, whose god had been Urizen, denies Tharmas, and, since Urizen is now apparently dead, proclaims himself god of the fallen world: 'But now I am all powerful Los & Urthona is but my shadow' (E 325; K 298). Enitharmon charges Tharmas with the destruction of Urizen's 'sweet world', and he separates her from Los. At this point Blake introduces the Spectre of Urthona, whose union with Los in Night VII will mark one of the turning-points in the narrative, making possible the building of Golgonooza. The Spectre of Urthona, the rationalistic and occasionally merely wilful aspect of Los, comes into prominence when Los is separated from his female emanation Enitharmon. Los as the Spectre of Urthona might be thought of as man without woman or man cut off from his feminine aspect, or possibly man without consciousness of the state of Beulah. This spectre could be identified with Los's abstract maleness apart from the mitigating influence of femaleness and its potentially creative force.

After a colloquy in which the Spectre recalls with Tharmas yet another version of the Fall, Tharmas asserts his power over all and commands the Spectre to help Los bind Urizen. Los now reappears and begins to bind the chains as Enitharmon laments, and the narrative picks up the story of his work from *The Book of Urizen*. After the binding of Urizen is finished, there is again a vision of the Council of God and of Luvah's robes of blood. But this time the presiding vision is not of Jesus in the robes but of Man or Albion: Blake has modulated his symbol cluster to emphasize the humanity of Jesus. The daughters of Beulah recognize that Jesus must appear in human form because they are 'weak women' to whose limited understanding Jesus must make Himself comprehensible.

The Saviour sets 'limits' on the Fall so that man can remain regenerable. Blake's concept of limits is probably a parody of the limits or 'fluxions', in Newtonian calculus, in which mathematical computations are based on fictional divisions that approach a limit of zero and are so small as not to have quantity, 'ghosts', as Bishop Berkeley derisively termed them, 'of disappearing quantities'.[14] The limits are necessary so that man does not fall into 'non-entity', and they are 'the Limit of Opacity', or Satan, and 'the Limit of Contraction' or Adam. Divine humanity is completely translucent and expansive, without limits at that end of the scale. Satan is opaque, admitting none of the divine vision, and Adam, or the red clay of man's body, is the lower limit of humanity.

Los shrinks in terrors from his task and begins a grotesque spasmic dance that continues in the fifth Night.

The St Vitus dance of Los is 'Infected Mad' and may allude to the sort of religious frenzy which infected those who went to the shrine of St Thomas Aquinas for a cure. All nature joins in it, in a passage of remarkable imagery:

> Grim frost beneath & terrible snow linkd in a marriage chain
> Began a dismal dance. The winds around on pointed rocks
> Settled like bats innumerable ready to fly abroad[.]   (E 332; K 306)

The spasms have also been sexual, for Orc is now born—or rather Luvah has now been transformed into Orc, in a grim parody of the Incarnation:

> The Enormous Demons woke & howld around the new born king
> Crying Luvah King of Love thou art the King of rage & death[.]
>   (E 333; K 306)

The demons sing one of Blake's set pieces, this one calling for corporeal war. As in the earlier development of Orc, he is nurtured and bound down by Los, with the assistance now of the Spectre of Urthona. Orc grows to huge proportions, attended by the 'spirits of life' to encompass all of nature. Los and Enitharmon, leaving Golgonooza, which they had been trying to build, feel sorrow for Orc and try to release him, but his chains have taken root. Satiated with grief, they return to Golgonooza, and on the road Enitharmon experiences a sort of painful inner revelation in which her 'bright heart burst open',—a heart which Vala 'began to reanimate in bursting sobs'. Urizen now begins to feel the force of Orc and is led to lament the loss of the old days. At the political level, George III is regretting some of his mistakes, like the American war,[15] in an echo of the fifth stanza of 'The Tyger':

> I well remember for I heard the mild & holy voice
> Saying O light spring up & shine & I sprang up from the deep
> He gave to me a silver scepter & crownd me with a golden crown
> & said Go forth & guide my Son who wanders on the ocean
> I went not forth. I hid myself in black clouds of my wrath
> I calld the stars around my feet in the night of councils dark
> The stars threw down their spears & fled naked away We fell.
>   (E 337; K 310–11)

This Night ends with Urizen preparing to go to explore the world created for him, as in *The Book of Urizen*, but it also introduces the theme of the *sparagmos*, or tearing up the body of a god and distributing it in nature, which will become important in the imagery of the ninth Night, where the process is reversed. Urizen is associated with bread or the body and Luvah with wine or blood, in another recollection of the events precipitating the Fall that adds a further dimension to the narrative. This closing passage is enormously condensed; but it might be read as meaning that Urizen refused his horses to Jesus but gave them to Luvah instead with the thought of absorbing to himself man's passional nature as embodied in Luvah. Luvah, on his part, wanted to absorb Urizen as order.

> . . . thou gavest Urizen the wine of the Almighty
> For steeds of Light that they might run in thy golden chariot of
>   pride
> I gave to thee the Steeds I pourd the stolen wine
> And drunken with the immortal draught fell from my throne
> sublime[.]   (E 337; K 311)

In Night VI Urizen explores his dens, encountering three 'terrific women', his daughters, whom he curses. Tharmas hears their scream and begins to respond but Urizen freezes the waves of his watery world. Again Tharmas wants to die but cannot. Meanwhile Urizen writes in his books of laws and wanders, eventually falling to a void, where he dies and is physically regenerated in the cyclical processes of nature. His travels take him into the physical heavens of 'rocky masses frowning in the abysses revolving erratic' in his ruined world. In an attempt to bring order to the erratic movement of this world, he often sits to 'regulate his books'. And he creates 'vortexes'—the whirling systems of motion which Descartes had postulated as the organizing motion of cosmic particles that conglomerated into planets, stars, and comets and whose movement he had described. Blake's idea of the vortex appears at crucial points in *Milton* and in 'The Mental Traveller', where it is used to symbolize a state of consciousness: passing from one vortex to another is like passing from one system of consciousness and perception to another, and in doing so one sees the vortex just passed roll up into globular forms. In *The Four Zoas* the vortexes are perhaps closer to their Cartesian source, as cosmic systems, or perhaps solar systems.[16] Granted a Urizenic world, they are necessary to organize it. Urizen's world is chaotic without them, and he can find no resting place where they do not operate. Indeed, some of them are providentially formed for him 'on high'.

As a god should, Urizen tries to transcend the whirling systems and get outside all systems, but he cannot:

> I thought perhaps to find an End a world beneath of voidness
> Whence I might travel round the outside of this Dark confusion
> When I bend downward bending my head downward into the deep
> Tis upward all which way soever I my course begin
> But when A Vortex formd on high by labour & sorrow & care
> And weariness begins on all my limbs then sleep revives
> My wearied spirits waking then tis downward all which way
> So ever I my spirits turn no end I find of all[.]   (E 342; K 317)

Without the organizing vortexes, his journey seems uphill all the way, and he can rest only in a vortex, within which travel becomes easier.

The imagery used to describe his world is full of echoes from Burnet's ruined world after the flood, which had occurred in Night III. Burnet had described the postdeluvian world as a 'great Ruine . . . lying in its rubbish' the inside of which is 'generally broken and hollow', full of 'holes Caverns, and strange subterranean passages'.[17] Urizen fixes his foot, as of a compass, and sets out to rebuild the world. In this image and in his earlier peering down into the abyss there are allusions to his appearance as The Ancient of Days with a compass in the frontispiece to *Europe*. He too digs in the subterranean depths of the ruined earth.

After attempting to organize his world into vortexes, moving from one to another and like a spider, weaving a web from one to another, he reaches the climax of his trip at the cave of Urthona. He encounters the 'Shadow of Urthona' as a vast armed spectre. Fifty-two armies, representing the counties of England and Wales, rise up round the spectre, as do his sons. He decides to retire into his web, shaking it as he goes, and sending a comet through the vortexes, down to Urthona's vale, where it flies round Orc, picks up an energy opposed to Urizen's, and returns through the vortexes back to Urizen, 'gorgd with blood' (E 345; K 320). As Night VI ends, Urizen's massy globes roll in their vortexes, and 'oerwheel' the 'dismal squadrons' of Urthona.

Night VII presents a special problem, because there are two versions of it. The version called 'a' and given first in sequence in the Erdman text is probably later and a replacement of the earlier one. Here Urizen descends to, but not into, the cave of Orc, whose fires he attempts to cool with his snows—as Satan will try to cool

Milton's brain later—and the Banyan tree of mystery grows up and envelops him. A colloquy of confrontation occurs between him and Orc, and Urizen reads from his books proclaiming himself god. He counsels Satanic policy cast hypocritically in the rhetoric of moral duty:

> Compell the poor to live upon a Crust of bread by soft mild arts
> Smile when they frown frown when they smile & when a man
>   looks pale
> With labour & abstinence say he looks healthy & happy
> And when his children sicken let them die there are enough
> Born even too many & our Earth will be overrun
> Without these arts[.]   (E 348; K 323)

Orc curses his 'cold hypocrisy', and recalls his original actions as Luvah. Urizen then recognizes Orc as Luvah and fears him. Under the influence of Urizen's moral virtue, Orc begins to assume a serpent body, and Urizen crucifies him on the tree of mystery, in another modulation of the symbolic cluster of Jesus in Luvah's robes of blood: Urizen feels the threat to his divinity comes from Luvah, who in his scheme of existence can be identified with Jesus, because to redeem man Jesus must identify himself with the dying god aspect of Luvah and suffer death. Urizen recognizes Orc as Luvah, and, when Orc assumes the serpentine form, Urizen naturally has to crucify him. Jesus Himself will be crucified in the next Night, and his mantle of Luvah, in which he has appeared throughout the poem, will separate from him. But here Urizen is mistaking the mantle for Jesus, in associating Jesus with Orc through the association with Luvah.

Events at this point follow so thick as to defy brief commentary. A new version of Enitharmon, a 'Shadow of Enitharmon', appears, is wooed by the Spectre of Urthona, and their union yields a version of Vala: they both recount the story of the original Fall. But the crucial event in this Night is Los's embrace of his Spectre and Enitharmon. He does this through pity, which here becomes not divisive but reunifying. When the union of Los with his Spectre and with Enitharmon occurs, they can begin to build Golgonooza, the city of art. Some of the imagery of this building refers to William and Catherine Blake etching and colouring:

> And first he drew a line upon the walls of shining heaven
> And Enitharmon tincturd it with beams of blushing love[.]
>   (E 356; K 332)

And the Night ends with a mood of forgiveness and love:

> Startled was Los he found his Enemy Urizen now
> In his hands. he wonderd that he felt love & not hate
> His whole soul loved him he beheld him an infant
> Lovely breathd from Enitharmon he trembled within himself[.]
> (E 357; K 332)

In Night VIII the Fall reaches its nadir on the limit of contraction, where the Council of God meets in its consolidated form as Jesus. But reaching the nadir or lower limit also marks the beginning of resurrection, as Albion, beginning to wake, sneezes. In this night error apparently triumphs, to gain ascendancy through the crucifixion of Christ and the emergence of a triumphant Rahab, or moral virtue as the Whore of Babylon; but the effect of this is to reveal error clearly and hence to set the stage for the climactic stripping off of inhuman excrescences in the astonishing imaginative energy of the apocalypse in the last Night. Night VIII is therefore the darkest part of the night before the blaze of glory in the 'harvest and vintage of nations' that follows.

The statement of the subject of *The Four Zoas* on the opening page announced it to be Los's 'fall into Division & his Resurrection to Unity' (E 297; K 264). In the earlier Nights, Los had indeed fallen, but in the seventh Night he had been partially resurrected to unity in embracing his Spectre. In the opening of Night VIII both he and Enitharmon perceive the divine vision:

> Then Los said I behold the Divine Vision thro the broken Gates
> Of thy poor broken heart astonished melted into Compassion &
>   Love
> And Enitharmon said I see the Lamb of God upon Mount Zion
> Wondring with love & Awe they felt the divine hand upon them[.]
> (E 357; K 341)

The vision of the Saviour, who has presided over all the action in the poem, now becomes more intense to them and envelops them in a new 'vortex':

> For whether they lookd upward they saw the Divine Vision
> Or whether they lookd downward still they saw the Divine Vision
> Surrounding them on all sides beyond sin & death & hell[.]
> (E 358; K 342)

In Night VIII the recurring image of Jesus in Luvah's robes of blood is brought to its climax. First Urizen sees it but, not being able to understand vision, totally fails to grasp its significance:

> When Urizen saw the Lamb of God clothed in Luvahs robes
> Perplexd & terrifid he Stood tho well he knew that Orc
> Was Luvah But he now beheld a new Luvah. Or One
> Who assumd Luvahs form & stood before him opposite[.]
> (E 358; K 342)

His concern is with Orc, who is 'augmenting times on times' in his serpentine form, in which he had been crucified in the preceding night. Now Urizen prepares for war. The battle itself takes on the form of a vast hermaphrodite called Satan. Next in the development of the image of Jesus and the robes of blood is its appearance to the nameless Shadowy Female, as the fallen Vala, who sees Jesus as the murderer of her Luvah. Then the Sons of Eden sing a lengthy song which tells of the efforts of Rahab, or moral virtue, to destroy the Lamb; but He puts off the robes of blood to redeem 'the spectre from their bonds' and awakes the sleepers in Ulro. Finally Christ is crucified, and Los takes the body to the sepulchre. But Rahab had cut the robes from the Saviour, and a revelation occurs, showing Rahab for what she is:

> But when Rahab had cut off the Mantle of Luvah from
> The Lamb of God it rolld apart, revealing to all in heaven
> And all on Earth the Temple & the Synagogue of Satan & Mystery
> Even Rahab is all her turpitude[.]   (E 365; K 350)

Other revelations follow. Los reveals himself to Rahab, tells her that he too had in his fallen condition 'pierced the Lamb of God in pride and wrath', and names his generations, that she may repent. A long catalogue of names follows. Here Blake through Los supplies a condensed summary of the doctrine of 'states' as distinguished from individuals; a character sketch of Satan as gaining power by the 'mild arts' he will show in *Milton*; and he concludes with an account of the 'seven eyes of God' mentioned earlier, ending with Jesus. Rahab departs burning with pride and revenge and Urizen suddenly beholds 'Reveald before the face of heaven his secret holiness' and is astonished in the literal sense of the word, stupefied by a stony vapour, as is everyone else. He embraces the Shadowy Female, as the only principle of life in the presence of death; and this leads to a further revelation in which all things are bound in a 'living Death'—in which they can be known and cast off in a recognition of the Divine Lamb:

> Thus in a living Death the nameless shadow all things bound
> All mortal things made permanent that they may be put off
> Time after time by the Divine Lamb who died for all
> And all in him died. & put off all mortality[.]   (E 368; K 353)

Ahania and Enion lament, and Los hears and takes the body of the Lamb from the cross to the sepulchre. Rahab triumphs over all. Satan, apparently taking this crucial point in history as marking an apocalypse of the antichrist, burns Mystery, essential to his religion but now about to be exposed; he plans to form from her ashes another mystery. But the ashes begin 'to animate' as Deism, which to Blake was not merely a religion without revelation but the consolidation of all rationalized religion whatever, from the time of Babylon onwards. And the Night ends with that, as a sort of unresolved cadence leading to the finale in Night IX.

Now the apocalypse in Night IX suddenly begins, with the resurrection of Jesus beside Los and Enitharmon, who are building Jerusalem in tears. But Jerusalem is not to be built like Golgonooza. Under the influence of Jesus, Los abruptly reaches to the sun and moon and pulls them down 'cracking the heavens across from immense to immense' to 'a mighty sound articulate' of trumpets calling everyone to awake. And we are off on one of the most astonishing *tours de force* in literature to which the briefly superficial commentary that might be given here would be a great impertinence. To anyone who has read through the preceding Nights of this marvellous poem with sympathetic understanding, the events of the apocalypse will perhaps be clear enough. The Last Judgment, which Blake thought of at one level as being an 'overwhelming of bad art and science', is the harvest and vintage of nations, conducted in general by Los. The effects, not surprisingly, are not always pleasant to individuals undergoing the vintage in having the husks of error separated from their human wine: 'the Human Grapes Sing not nor dance / They howl & writhe in shoals of torment' (E 389; K 377). The encrustations of six thousand years of the fallen world are not easily removed. The black African, having the least error to get rid of, has an easier time of it (E 388; K 375). Finally the zoas are regenerated, are altered, and the work ends serenely with the departure of corporeal war and its replacement by the intellectual war:

> ... Urthona rises from the ruinous walls
> In all his ancient strength to form the golden armour of science
> For intellectual War The war of swords departed now
> The dark Religions are departed & sweet Science reigns[.]
>   (E 392; K 379)

8 | The last prophecies

The appropriate attitude for a poet who would expand men's vision in a fallen world and help bring about an apocalypse through an overwhelming of bad art and science is that expressed by the Bard in the next work completed by Blake in illuminated printing, *Milton*: 'Mark well my words! they are of your eternal salvation' (E 96; K 482). Not many people marked Blake's words, and he probably recognized that he could not reach an audience with a work like *The Four Zoas*, marvellous though it is. The need to try to reach an audience and speak directly to them as a 'true orator', as he called himself in the Preface to *Jerusalem*, was borne in on him during his three years with William Hayley in Felpham and dramatically revealed to him in his actually being tried for the high crime of treason early in 1804. The visionary scheme of *The Four Zoas*, though it brought into a coherent whole all the pieces of a mythology that he had been developing for some years, finally turned out to be rather too comprehensive to express what had to be said by a Bard for the salvation of his audience.

Accordingly, at some point in his Felpham sojourn, very likely unknown to Hayley, Blake began *Milton*, a long work in illuminated printing that analysed human character into three categories as classes of men, not zoas, and showed the great poet of England and Blake's idol, Milton, who had been partly drawn into the starry wheels of rationalized theology, come down from his unhappy situation in heaven and cast off all in him that was not human and derived from the divine imagination. Blake addressed directly in a preface the 'Young Men of the New Age', painters, sculptors, architects, calling on them to embrace a new aesthetic as an essential act in bringing about the new Jerusalem in England and dedicating himself to this enterprise in the famous prefatory lyric:

And did those feet in acient time.
Walk upon Englands mountains green:
And was the holy Lamb of God,
On Englands pleasant pastures seen!

And did the Countenance Divine,
Shine forth upon our clouded hills?
And was Jerusalem builded here,
Among these dark Satanic Mills?

Bring me my Bow of burning gold:
Bring me my Arrows of desire:
Bring me my Spear: O clouds unfold!
Bring me my Chariot of fire!

I will not cease from Mental Fight,
Nor shall my Sword sleep in my hand:
Till we have built Jerusalem,
In Englands green & pleasant Land.   (E 95; K 481–82)

There is no ambiguity about these questions, as there are about those in 'The Tyger'; they are a rhetorical summons to action.

Probably conceived with *Milton* and begun shortly after it, was yet another work of true oratory, a huge epic twice as long as *Milton* and addressed, in prefaces to its four chapters, to: The Public, Jews, Deists, and Christians. Both works are dated 1804 on their title-pages, though no copy of *Milton* is known before 1808 and no copy of *Jerusalem* before 1818–20. The two works are related, and the prefatory lyric just quoted anticipates in its imagery of mills, the mental fight, and archery some key passages in *Jerusalem* while, as the title indicates, the later epic is concerned with the building of the city of God.

As much as he wanted to reach an audience directly, Blake failed until a century after his death. The only public notice of the late work in his lifetime appeared in a humorous squib in the *London Magazine*, by a Thomas Wainewright, a pupil of Fuseli, who described it as 'an ancient, newly discovered, illuminated manuscript, which has to name "Jerusalem the Emanation of the Giant Albion!!!" It contains a good deal anent one "*Los*", who, it appears, is now, and hath been from the creation, the *sole* and fourfold dominator of the celebrated city of *Golgonooza*!'[1] The irony of this account was probably intended light-heartedly, for Wainewright was a friend of Blake's. Unfortunately, he was also later a murderer and forger.

Both works do contain a good deal about Los, for Blake pretty much dropped the scheme of the four zoas in them. In *Milton* Urizen is identified as Satan in the opening story told by the Bard and as one of the three classes of men, and he is mentioned in *Jerusalem*, as are the other zoas. In the last great epics Blake wanted to humanize his work by focusing on a historical cultural hero and to make it more concrete by adapting his myth specifically to the geography of the British Isles—or perhaps the other way round. Again, though he retains elements and even transposes passages from *The Four Zoas*, he shifts the context of his myth to take in more traditional symbols like Satan. Orc and Tharmas become rather irrelevant. Albion and Jerusalem, of course, are of central importance, and Los, Enitharmon, Vala, and, to a lesser extent, Luvah and Urizen remain, as does the Spectre of Urthona.

Milton and *Jerusalem* are large works in every sense. *Milton* consists of a total of fifty-one plates richly illuminated and *Jerusalem* of one hundred. Any attempt to do more than give each a cursory glance here would be impossible.

Milton is a theodicy, as the epigraph 'To Justify the Ways of God to Men' on the title-page clearly indicates, but Blake has a different conception of the ways of God to men than his hero had in *Paradise Lost*. Most of the work is devoted to showing this by Milton's going to annihilation of the 'selfhood' in him, struggling to give form to Satan so that he may be known, and liberating his poetic genius from the encrustations of classical art and rationalized religion. God being imagination and knowable by the poetic genius, the ways of God to men are self-evidently justified through a liberation of the imagination. Perception of being by means of the imagination also reveals that human life is characterized by the Contraries.

In making Milton the central figure of his poem, Blake is not 'correcting' but celebrating him. As Florence Sandler suggests, 'Only Milton—enthusiast, prophet and revolutionary—can be the Awakener of Albion in these latter days, the Elijah whose Second Coming signifies that Eschaton [the end or last thing] has arrived and the Great Harvest and Vintage of Nations now begins.'[2] But, as Blake had said in *The Marriage*, Milton had to some extent been drawn in by satanic theology, and the true poet and prophet had to be revealed and redeemed. Accordingly, the poem shows Milton going to purge himself:

I will go down to self annihilation and eternal death,
Lest the Last Judgment come & find me unannihilate
And I be siez'd & giv'n into the hands of my own Selfhood.
  (E 107; K 495)

The crucial—though confusing—opening story of Rintrah, Palamabron, and Satan (Urizen) makes the point that any man including
Blake himself is susceptible to the mild blandishments of Satan.
For Satan in Blake is not an operatic basso version appearing in
flashes of fire and hence easily recognizable but the mildest and
most seductive of characters, indeed a 'corporeal friend' like William
Hayley, who could be a 'spiritual enemy'.[3] And because Blake
identified himself so strongly with Milton, the purging of Milton
by annihilating the satanic selfhood in him is to some extent
therefore also a purging of Blake himself in preparation for his
part in bringing about the apocalypse.

In the Bard's opening song that delineates the three classes of
men always on earth, Blake uses two characters from earlier work
who appear as the sons of Los in *The Four Zoas*, Rintrah and
Palamabron. Los has four sons, described later in *Milton* in a way
to suggest that something of the division of the human soul in the
zoas is continued in them, in a more humanized second generation
of zoas, as it were. Los speaks:

    . . . I the Fourth Zoa am also set
    The Watchman of Eternity, the Three are not! & I am preserved
    Still my four mighty ones are left to me in Golgonooza
    Still Rintrah fierce, and Palamabron mild & piteous
    Theotormon filld with care, Bromion loving Science[.]
      (E 118; K 508)

The other figure in the song is Satan, who is identified with Urizen,
also represented as a son of Los.

Blake's idea of the Contraries was largely suspended in *The
Four Zoas*, but in *Milton* and also in *Jerusalem* it reassumes a great
deal of importance, for the three classes of men are 'the Two
Contraries & the Reasoning Negative' (E 98; K 484). Rintrah
represents the active Contrary that often takes the form of wrath.
Palamabron is the passive Contrary and mild pity, representing the
ordinary good man. Because Palamabron shares the quality of
mildness with Satan, he is particularly susceptible to seduction by
Satan. Satan is not a Contrary but a Negation, who merely denies.

The wrathful energetic class of Contraries are called the 'Reprobate' because that is the way ordinary society perceives them, and the gentle pitying passive Contraries are called the 'Redeemed' for the same reason. The Negations are called the 'Elect', in an ironic thrust at the self-righteous predestinarianism that Blake so abominated.

Distinguishing Contraries from Negations is a matter of transcendent importance. In the climatic speech of the poem, Milton makes this explicit to his emanation Ololon, who has been 'scatter'd thro' the deep' (E 95; K 481) and who has now joined him:

> But turning toward Ololon in terrible majesty Milton
> Replied. Obey thou the Words of the Inspired Man
> All that can be annihilated must be annihilated
> That the Children of Jerusalem may be saved from slavery
> There is a Negation, & there is a Contrary
> The Negation must be destroyd to redeem the Contraries
> The Negation is the Spectre; the Reasoning Power in Man
> This is a false Body: an Incrustation over my Immortal
> Spirit; a Selfhood, which must be put off & annihilated alway
> To cleanse the Face of my Spirit by Self-examination.
>   (E 141; K 532–3)

But such self-examination is very difficult because in the fallen world the identities of the contraries and the reasoning negative have become confused. So the main burden of the Bard's song in *Milton* is to show, by a rather confusing narrative, how that confusion came about. The story contains many complicating details; but essentially it relates a story parallel to the narratives of the 'dread day' in *The Four Zoas* when the identities and functions of Urizen and Luvah were confused and the eternal cyclical processes of Eden were drawn down and contaminated, to become the ordinary cycles of the sun and moon in the processes of nature. For again there is a confusion of functions, this time between Urizen and Palamabron.

Following the order of plates in the last copy of *Milton*,[4] we get first the account of the material creation of the human body through 'seven ages' that first appeared in *The Book of Urizen* and again in *The Four Zoas*. Then Satan is born, the youngest of the Sons of Los and Enitharmon. Los prepares to give him an appropriate form, as the 'Miller of Eternity made subservient to the Great Harvest' and 'Prince of the Starry Wheels' (E 97; K 483). But

Satan wants to remain unidentified and tries to refuse any form, because he aspires to Eternity and wants to take over the function of the passive contrary, Palamabron. Los, however tells him that everyone ought to keep his proper place, that 'Every Man's wisdom is peculiar to his own Individuality' (E 97; K 483), and Satan's individuality must not be that of the giver of eternal forms but that of the corporeal workmaster and engineer. His is not the creative mercy of the passive Contrary, which he can understand only as 'pity'.

Satan 'trembling obey'd, weeping along the way' but only temporarily. Shortly, by means of his mildness he imposes on both Los and Palamabron and succeeds in taking over Palamabron's harrowing by nagging:

> He soft intreated Los to give to him Palamabrons station;
> For Palamabron returnd with labour wearied every evening
> Palamabron oft refus'd; and as often Satan offer'd
> His service till by repeated offers and repeated intreaties
> Los gave to him the Harrow of the Almighty[.] . . . (E 99; K 486)

The results are disastrous, for everything is in chaos. Palamabron is angry but bottles up his wrath, though he does call Los and Satan to view the damage. Satan again weeps, 'mildly cursing Palamabron,' and accuses him 'of crimes Himself had wrought' (E 100; K 487). Los is uncertain what to do because Satan has no understanding of his having done anything wrong.

Not all the effects of the exchange of tasks are yet known. Satan returns to his mills to discover that the servants of the mills have been driven into madness and drunkenness by the heady influence of the eternal Palamabron:

> . . . Los beheld
> The servants of the Mills drunken with wine and dancing wild
> With shouts and Palamabrons songs, rending the forests green
> With ecchoing confusion, tho' the Sun was risen on high.
>   (E 101; K 488)

Filled with remorse, Los makes the curious gesture of putting his left sandal on his head, perhaps symbolizing the topsy turvy confusion, and declares a day of mourning.

But the confusion has gone too far to be rectified, and chaos and contention reign, as Theotormon and Bromion side with Satan.

Rintrah, the wrathful energetic contrary, alone recognizes that Los's solutions are but temporary ones and turns on Satan the just wrath that everyone thus far has avoided. As always, Satan tries 'soft dissimulation of friendship', but Rintrah is not susceptible to it. Now Satan turns as 'angry & red' as Rintrah is. He then murders his friend Thulloh[5] and stands 'terrible' over his traditional adversary, Michael, who is also there. And then he weeps.

Palambrom calls down

> . . . a Great Solemn Assembly
> That he who will not defend Truth, may be compelled to
> Defend a Lie, that he may be snared & caught & taken[.]
>   (E 102; K 489)

Palamabron appeals to Eden for a judgment and gets a very strange one: 'Lo! it fell on Rintrah and his rage', not on Satan. And here the confusion of identities gets fixed in Satan coming to be known as the fiery character of tradition, as the reprobate. For Rintrah's wrath, which Satan had taken on,

> . . . flam'd high & furious in Satan against Palamabron
> Till it became a proverb in Eden. Satan is among the Reprobate.
>   (E 102; K 489)

Los rages on a grand scale, displacing the universe. And Satan, not satisfied and still 'flaming with Rintrah's fury hidden beneath his own mildness', accuses Palamabron, creates seven deadly sins, and proclaims himself god, as his bosom grows 'Opake against the Divine Vision'. At last Los and Enitharmon recognize him as the fallen Urizen.

The judgment, however, was an unjust one; for not only was the wrath of Rintrah condemned but Satan was given an association with the active energetic contraries—the misconception that Blake had set out to correct in *The Marriage*, where, of course, a real Satan did not exist. How could a judgment of a Solemn Assembly of Eden be so much in error? The answer is that it was providential, forced on Eden by error and given in order to preserve for man the possibility of regeneration through the self-sacrifice of the great redeeming act of the forgiveness of sins:

> And it was enquir'd: Why in a Great Solemn Assembly
> The Innocent should be condemn'd for the Guilty? Then an
>   Eternal rose

Saying. If the Guilty should be condemn'd, he must be an
  Eternal Death
And one must die for another throughout all Eternity.
  (E 104; K 491)

Moreover, Satan cannot be redeemed, but he must be 'new Created continually' so that he can be known.

At the last, in the apocalypse, even the elect will be at least partly redeemed and will recognize that they exist by providence:

  . . . We behold it is of Divine
  Mercy alone! of Free Gift and Election that we live.
  Our Virtues & Cruel Goodnesses, have deserv'd Eternal Death.
  (E 106; K 491)

Satan will recognize the irony of his having called those of his class 'the elect': he will know that he has indeed been the elect of heaven, chosen, however, not by a harsh and self-righteous pre-destination but by a merciful providence that forgives his sins.

The fuller meaning of all this confusion of identities comes out toward the very end of the Bard's song, where Enitharmon creates a new space to 'protect Satan from punishment', and the Assembly gives time to the space, sending, in succession, the 'seven eyes of God' to guard the space, the last being Jesus. When Jesus comes, 'the Body of Death was perfected in hypocritic holiness', and He is known as a reprobate: 'He died as a Reprobate. he was Punish'd as a Transgressor!' (E 106; K 494).

The corollary of this great confusion is that, while Jesus was crucified as a Reprobate, He came subsequently to be worshiped as one of the Elect. For Satan's influence is pervasive because it is not recognized for what it is, Satan generally being thought to be one of the Reprobate, whereas in fact he is one of the Elect. Even a very great prophetic poet like Milton was to some extent misled by this confusion and, as Blake had said in *The Marriage*, 'wrote in fetters when he wrote of Angels & God' because he was intellectually committed to the religion of the Elect (E 35; K 150) and was implicated in a corporeal war fought partly on religious issues. Accordingly, when the Bard's song disturbs the assembly to which he sang it and the very foundations are shaken 'in doubtfulness', the Bard takes refuge in Milton's bosom, completing the identification of Milton and Blake. Milton then rises from the 'heavens of Albion ardorous' and announces that he will purge the Satanic selfhood from himself: 'I go to Eternal Death'. He wonders, 'What do I here before the Judgment? without my Emanation?' and he concludes, 'I in my Selfhood am that Satan: I am that Evil One' (E 107; K 495).

The Bard's song takes up the first thirteen plates of the work, about one-third. The main action in the remaining two-thirds concerns Milton's journey to Eternal Death to find Satan and his return in 'terrible majesty' to be reunited with his emanation Ololon. This action extends to the end of the work. But there are other elements and sections as well. One is the descent of Ololon to Eternal Death in search of Milton, which is simultaneous with part of Milton's journey and which, of course, ends with their reunion. The fact that Ololon's quest for Milton brings her to Blake's own cottage door in Felpham, where her reunion with Milton occurs, indicates another element in the work. Milton has been travelling not only through the chaotic universes on his way to find Satan; he has in a strange way been moving forward in time, until he enters Blake's foot. Since Los the prophetic spirit is associated with the feet, Milton's entering Blake's foot suggests that the prophetic power of Milton, which perhaps he failed to use fully during his own lifetime, is now being transferred to Blake. To put it a shade reductively, Blake shows Milton as passing on the inspiration of the prophet-poet to him. This work is unusual in Blake's being a character in it himself, not only through the persona of the Bard but also directly, in his association with Milton and with Los. The characters of his myth literally come down to earth in Felpham. Still another element, or in this case an inserted section covering plates 22 to 29, concerns the works of Los in building Golgonooza and giving form to the fallen world by the 'mathematic power' he is compelled to exercise.

Earlier, I suggested that Blake wanted to communicate. The complexity and richness of *Milton* might raise a question as to how much. But a further question is how much is there for a poet-prophet to communicate who is striving to bring about a fundamental change in man's modes of thought? In *Milton*, as in other works, Blake really tries to give his reader as much information as he possibly can, without expressing the burden of his work in the terms of the entrenched systems that he believes must be destroyed. It may be that he tries too hard, interspersing his narrative with too much visionary doctrine and cosmology. But he had dedicated himself to 'Mental Fight' in the opening lyric, and was further impelled in 1804 by the strongest personal reasons, in his association with Hayley and in the trial.

In a short prefatory lyric to Chapter Four of *Jerusalem*, Blake characterizes the method of his works:

> I give you the end of a golden string,
>> Only wind it into a ball:
> It will lead you in at Heavens gate,
>> Built in Jerusalems wall. (E 229; K 716)

The end of the string in *Milton* can be the plot. The Bard's song tells a story of how the identities of the two contrary classes of men came to be confused with that of Satan, who belongs in a different class, and the actions of Satan in the narrative begin to define his character. Then Milton, moved by the Bard's song, determines to purge the satanic aspect of his own character as he has seen it defined for him in the events of the narrative. He is in Heaven, of course, and has an eternal identity, in which he is lying on a golden couch, while two other aspects of his character descend to Hell to find Satan so that his satanic aspect can be purged from him. A confrontation ensues in which Milton tries to make the insidious Satan take on a bodily form so that he can henceforth be recognized, while Satan, who is opposed to vigorous mental activity, tries to quench Milton's hot brain with ice water. In the meantime, his emanation or feminine counterpart, Ololon, who has been separated from him, learns of his journey to Eternal Death or Hell and in remorse for having driven him out begins to search for him. Both Milton and Ololon are instructed in certain doctrines essential for them to know if they are to be free of the satanic influence. Among these is the need to distinguish individuals from states that individuals may fall into, so that individuals may not be condemned for their actions in such states and can be forgiven their sins in emulation of the forgiveness of Jesus. Another is the need to distinguish the contraries that inform all of life and function harmoniously but vigorously in a mental war, from negations which would deny everything but themselves and create destructive corporeal war. A final confrontation between Milton and Satan occurs, in which Milton, now free of any satanic influence, can vigorously reject Satan even though Satan insists he is god, as in effect he has been. Ololon, meeting Milton now, recognizes that she, as his feminine counterpart, is his creative contrary, and her satanic aspect, represented as self-seeking femaleness called 'virginity', departs. All this time, and indeed for six thousand years, the prophetic spirit, Los has been giving form to a world which would have been chaotic had Satan complete sway over it. And the prophetic spirits of Los and Milton now inspire Blake. Since Milton, the very great poet-prophet has now, as it were, made his appearance in modern times at Blake's cottage, where the action ends, the time for the great change in the apocalypse is at hand.

The preceding attempt at a plot summary leaves out an enormous amount, of course. But reading *Milton* for the narrative takes one into its ideas, because it is a good narrative. And doing that starts the process of rolling up the golden string.

Milton is, like *Paradise Regained* on which it is structurally modelled, a narrative work. *Jerusalem* is not, and its unusual structure has frustrated and tantalized critics, some of whom have supplied 'keys' to it, a tendency in Blake criticism that has fortunately been largely discarded. Harold Bloom's suggestion that *Jerusalem* represents a 're-creation in English terms of the work of Hebraic prophecy seems to me a very useful one and is certainly supported by the fact that it is the most explicitly biblical of Blake's works. It develops through its four chapters, addressed in turn to the Public, to the Jews, to the Deists, and to the Christians, with some sense of a succession of events, not exactly as a narrative but rather in four stages that are relevant, but with some overlapping, to the four audiences addressed. To the extent that there is a narrative, it involves the weakening of Albion in the first two chapters especially, the growth of the power of Albion's malevolent sons, the appearance of Jesus, and finally the Apocalypse. Again, as in all the later works, Los, in his relations with his spectre and his emanation Enitharmon, assumes great importance.

Another structural feature of *Jerusalem* is the presiding imagery of furnaces and wheels which Blake insistently develops in the first chapter and which recurs throughout. The twelve evil Sons of Albion are first introduced as revolving 'most mightily / Upon the furnaces of Los' and they continue to revolve in 'starry wheels' all through the poem, either being explicitly shown to do this with the stars or suggested as doing this by verbs of rotation. As we noted in discussing *The Four Zoas*, cyclical motion in Blake's cosmos is not in itself bad, and Eternity itself operates on benignly cyclical principles. But the starry wheels of abstract system founded in a material creation produce a rotational system that moves everything within by compulsion, like a train of gears.

Opposed to the starry wheels are the furnaces of Los. Again, furnaces are of two kinds. One is represented by the 'furnaces of affliction' in which the fallen Luvah was sealed, and these represent the physical body. The other kind is the furnace of creative activity which has to be kept hot for Los, the cosmic smith, in order to give what form he can to a falling world and also to build Golgonooza, the city of art. In Blake's own time, with the rapid development of machine production by factory wheels, the opposition between wheels and furnaces takes on a special significance as a contrast between industrial production, with some of its attendant social evils, and hand manufacture, in its etymological sense. The 'dark Satanic mills' in England's otherwise green and pleasant land certainly include factories. But all such mills become possible only under a philosophical system that can be symbolized by the imagery of starry wheels, which express all kinds of repression whatever.

The opposition of the presiding imagery of starry wheels is finally resolved at the very end of *Jerusalem*, on the 96th plate just before Albion precipitates the Apocalypse by shooting his mighty bow, when the furnaces (of affliction this time) become fountains and the stars burn up:

> So Albion spoke & threw himself into the furnaces of affliction.
> All was a vision, all a dream! The furnaces became
> Fountains of living waters flowing from the Humanity Divine.
> And all the cities of Albion rose from their slumbers, & all
> The sons & daughters of Albion on soft clouds waking from sleep;
> Soon all around remote the heavens burnt with flaming fires[.]
> (E 253; K 744)

On the very last plate, the benign planetary motion of Eternity is restored:

> All Human Forms identified even Tree Metal Earth & Stone. all
> Human Forms identified, living going forth & returning wearied
> Into the Planetary lives of Years Months Days & Hours reposing
> And then Awaking into his Bosom in the Life of Immortality.
> (E 256; K 747)

The planetary wheels within wheels in this passage and others connect the work with Ezekiel.

Blake's model for his starry wheels, of course, is in Newton's astronomy, as he understood it. But the wheels are conceived in a system that is much less abstract and one that lends itself to concrete visualization of a cosmology appropriate to poetic imagery. The form of the fallen life in which the starry wheels revolve has the form of the 'mundane shell', which we noted earlier. And it has compass points that Blake manipulates in showing the dislocations produced by the Fall. Both Blake and his readers are accustomed to thinking of compass points as being stationary, flatly projected on a map rather than on a globe, and it is sometimes hard to project them back to a sphere again. But it seems to me that we miss something in Blake's cosmology in *Jerusalem* with its whirling systems, and elsewhere, if we have the flat projection in mind.

In *Jerusalem* more than anywhere else, Blake embraces the world of Generation, calling it, through Los, 'holy Generation [Image] of regeneration' (E 149; K 626), and he makes creation a merciful act. Creation moves from east to west, as is shown in the poem prefatory to Chapter Four, reminiscent of Thomas Vaughan's 'The World.' But the satanic wheels of natural religion go the other way:

> I stood among my valleys of the south
> And saw a flame of fire, even as a Wheel
> Of fire surrounding all the heavens: it went
> From west to east against the current of
> Creation and devoured all things in its loud
> Fury & thundering course round heaven & earth[.]   (E 230; K 717)

The speaker asks what is the wheel and is told 'It is the wheel of religion'. And he asks, 'Is this the law of Jesus, / This terrible devouring sword turning every way?' and is told that 'Jesus died because he strove / Against the current of this wheel', in other words in the direction of creation.

The compass points of north and south present no problem, for Blake's cosmos rotates on a polar axis. Before the Fall, Urthona was in the north, Urizen in the south, Luvah in the east, and Tharmas in the west. And the rotational direction of the providential creation under the control of Jesus is *toward* the west, toward the 'gate' of Tharmas through which man will pass to regeneration. The rotational direction is *from* the east, from the unfallen Luvah. After the Fall, Urizen, or Satan as he has now become, moves to the west and makes the rotation turn around, still going toward

Tharmas but not toward the western gate, because Tharmas has now moved to the east. The motion is not toward regeneration, but the other way, toward Eternal Death.

Blake ingeniously uses the change of rotation to create the corporeal sun and moon, in the prefatory poem already quoted. By the reversed rotation of the wheel of religion,

> . . . the Sun was rolld into an orb:
> By it the Moon faded into a globe,
> Travelling thro the night. . . . (E 230; K 717)

What were rings of light now are rolled up into spheres.

The starry wheels of the fallen world involve the twelve sons of Albion. In applying his myth of Albion to his native England, making Albion into a giant who encompasses the British Isles and whose cities are named and humanized in the work, Blake gives identities to Albion's malevolent sons. Prominent among them is Schofield, the soldier who made the deposition against Blake leading to his trial, and his fellow soldier, Cock, spelled Cox here. Also included are the brothers Hunt, represented as Hand because of the editorial mark they used in *The Examiner*, whose editorials had attacked Blake. Hayley appears as Hyle, perhaps Hayley pronounced with a cockney accent. Others are: Peachey, Bereton, and Quantock, who were justices at Blake's trial; Hutton, an officer of the court; Bowen, an attorney who may have been connected with the trial; and Coban, Kotope, and Slayd, who have not been clearly identified, though Bacon has been suggested for Coban, anagrammatically, in which case he would be the only Son of Albion who is not a contemporary. In being thus identified, the Sons represent the spiritual condition of England as Blake personally experienced it.

The matching twelve Daughters of Albion are not connected with contemporaries but are with a few exceptions legendary British princesses, their 'names anciently remembered, but now contemn'd as fictions' (E 146; K 624), representing the female will through the ages. The daughters are the emanations of the sons.

Albion is given geographical specificity by catalogues of the counties of England and Scotland. His friends are the cathedral cities, represented as individuals, notably Bath, who is quite certainly an actual individual, the Rev. Richard Warner, a clergyman and literary man of that city who spoke out in a sensational sermon against the war with France.

All this geographical specificity intensifies the traditional association of Albion with contemporary Britain. And in this work Blake also gives a fuller, more rounded portrait of Albion as the figure representing man—or Man. Whereas in *The Four Zoas*, Man or Albion was rather vaguely shown in brief scenes or glimpses, he appears more fully here. And Blake has again adjusted his myth so that Vala, who was in *The Four Zoas* a sort of seducer of Albion but also the emanation of Luvah, here becomes fully associated with Albion as another emanation of Albion along with Jerusalem, but a destructive one. Here Vala's luring Albion away from Jerusalem shows the Fall dramatized in human terms. Luvah no longer fits into this version of the story of Vala and appears only as one of the four raging fallen zoas who are mentioned from time to time.

Jerusalem also appears more fully as a woman in this more direct representation of the Albion-Jerusalem relationship. But the traditional association of Jerusalem as the city of God is also developed more fully. Jerusalem as woman, as emanation, is the consort of Albion; and literally as a city Jerusalem will become the civilized urban centre of 'England's green and pleasant land', at the apocalypse seen at the end of the work.

A good deal of the complexity of *Jerusalem* comes about because in it Blake combines, as fully as he can, not only the traditional mythology of Britain with the geography, politics, philosophy, and a host of other features of contemporary Britain, all coming to a focus in the figure of Albion. He also combines with all this various elements of the biblical tradition, not only in the figure of Jerusalem but in the visions of Ezekiel, reflected in the presiding imagery of wheels, and in the stories of Israel and Reuben. In addition, he casts all this together with the essential features of his own mythology centred in Los, together with his own cosmology and his own ontological ideas, like that of the eternal creative Contraries which the Sons of Albion pervert into destructive Negations. Moreover, through all this there is felt the redeeming presence of Jesus, as in *The Four Zoas*, becoming manifest in the third chapter, in a nativity in which Blake rejects the idea of the virgin birth as being not only unessential to the divinity of Jesus but as expressing a false doctrine (like that of glorifying the God of material creation) because it obscures the nature of divine mercy, in translating it literally into physical generation in sexual form.

Jerusalem is, as Northrop Frye has called it, a 'dehydrated epic'.[6]

It is tremendously condensed, and even the long catalogues of counties and cities are essential to Blake's purpose—though admittedly it is hard not to skip over them in reading. At one point Blake projected it as a work of twenty-eight chapters instead of the four we have—though that number of chapters would probably have subdivided the work rather than multiplied its length by seven. And its intensity and concentration are increased by the illuminations of the text, which form an essential ingredient in its structure, the wonderful full plate illustration of the crucifixion (plate 76), for instance, coming as a great climax to chapter three, and the themes of the work being developed even in the tiny figures which at first glance look like linear ornamentation in the margins. It has to be seen to be believed.

Despite its own kind of concentration, *The Four Zoas* is an expansive, imaginatively exuberant work, with an apocalyptic finale that reminds one of the finale of Beethoven's Ninth Symphony. It explodes with energy. To continue the metaphor, *Jerusalem* might be said to implode with a concentration of practically everything Blake ever thought or imagined; and no visionary interpretation of life has been as fully extended into every area of human activity as Blake's.

Notes

Chapter 1. Some biographical facts

1. E. M. Forster, 'An approach to Blake', *Spectator*, cxlviii (1932), 474.

2. Jean H. Hagstrum, *William Blake: Poet and Painter* (Chicago, 1964); Kathleen Raine, *Blake and Tradition*, 2 vols. (Princeton, 1968); David V. Erdman and John E. Grant, Eds., *Blake's Visionary Forms Dramatic* (Princeton).

3. For biographical information I draw heavily on G. E. Bentley Jr, *Blake Records* (Oxford, 1969), an invaluable compendium of contemporary records of Blake. I give page references only for quotations.

4. John Thomas Smith, *Nollekens and his Times* (1828), in Bentley, *Blake Records*, p. 457; also in Arthur Symons, *William Blake* (London, 1907), p. 360.

5. Alexander Gilchrist, *Life of William Blake* (London, 1945), pp. 31–2. This edition includes notes by Ruthven Todd.

6. Bentley, *Blake Records*, p. 24.

7. Smith in Bentley, *Blake Records*, p. 456.

8. Bentley, *Blake Records*, p. 25.

9. Gilchrist, p. 51.

10. Published in photographic facsimile, Ed. Geoffrey Keynes, as *The Notebook of William Blake Called the Rossetti Manuscript* (London, 1935). A new facsimile, *The Notebook of William Blake*, Ed. David V. Erdman and Donald K. Moore (London, 1973) gives by means of infra-red photography more of the text than could be read before, and also gives an accurate typographic facsimile of the text.

11. A facsimile of the MS and reproductions of the drawings have been published, Ed. G. E. Bentley Jr, William Blake, *Tiriel* (Oxford, 1967).

12. Bentley, *Blake Records*, p. 35.

13. *The Poetry and Prose of William Blake*, Ed. David V. Erdman (Garden City, N.Y., 1965), p. 600. Quotations from Blake are from the third printing, with revisions, 1968. Page references will also be given to *The Complete Writings of William Blake*, Ed. Geoffrey Keynes (London, 1966). Citations will be abbreviated, e.g., E 600; K 133, for this one.

14. *Collected Letters of Samuel Taylor Coleridge*, Ed. Earl Leslie Griggs (Oxford, 1956), I, 397.

15. David V. Erdman, *Blake: Prophet against Empire*, rev. ed. (Garden City, N.Y., 1969), 164.

16. In a poem to Blake by Hayley. See *The Letters of William Blake*, Ed. Geoffrey Keynes (Cambridge, Mass., 1970), p. 36. A just account of Blake's relationship with Hayley is given in Morchard Bishop (Oliver Stoner), *Blake's Hayley* (London, 1951).

17. The indictment, Rex *v.* Blake, in Bentley, *Blake Records*, p. 133. The main charge was technically sedition, not treason, though sedition could be extended to treason under the Treasonable Practices Act of 1795. Jacob Bronowski, in *William Blake, 1757–1827* (Harmondsworth, 1954), p. 117, believes that in the circumstances of 1804 Blake would 'hardly have been sentenced to as much as a year in prison'.

18. Bentley, *Blake Records*, p. 236.

19. ibid., p. 146.

20. ibid., p. 146.

21. ibid., p, 345

22. Letter to Gilchrist, 23 August 1855, in Gilchrist, pp. 301–04.

Chapter 2. *'Poetical Sketches' and other early works*

1. See Margaret Ruth Lowery, *Windows of the Morning* (New Haven, 1940) for a detailed study of these poems and their background.

2. Bentley, *Blake Records*, p. 457, Symons, p. 360.

3. Erdman, *Blake: Prophet*, pp. 20–2.

4. S. Foster Damon, *A Blake Dictionary* (Providence, Rhode Island, 1965), p. 229

5. Erdman, *Blake: Prophet*, pp. 72–3.

6. The suggestion for this identification is by Palmer Brown. See Erdman, *Blake: Prophet*, pp. 93–4n.

7. Martha W. England, 'Apprenticeship at the Haymarket?' in Erdman and Grant, Eds., *Visionary Forms Dramatic*, pp. 3–29, condensed from an essay in *Bulletin of the New York Public Library*, lxxii (1969), 440–64, 531–50.

Chapter 3. *Early works in 'Illuminated Printing'*

1. See Geoffrey Keynes, *Blake Studies*, rev. ed. (Oxford, 1971), pp. 122–9.

2. E 670; K 207–8.

3. E 151; K 629.

4. Francis Bacon, *Philosophical Works*, trans. Peter Shaw (London, 1733), II, 335–6.

5. Bacon, II, 332.

6. ibid., 333.

7. E 637; K 459.

8. E 511; K 750.

9. An extended and fundamentally important account of Blake's theory of perception is given in Northrop Frye, *Fearful Symmetry* (Boston, 1962), chapter I.

10. E 555; K 617.

11. E 53; K 199.

12. E 555; K 617.

13. Quoted in Bentley, *Blake Records*, p. 252.

14. E 490; K 183.

15. E 763; K 380.

16. Quoted in Hoxie Neale Fairchild, *The Noble Savage* (New York, 1928), p. 474.

17. For details see my 'Fact and symbol in "The Chimney Sweeper" of Blake's *Songs of Innocence*', *Bulletin of the New York Public Library*, lviii (1964), 249–56.

18. Ursula Vaughan Williams as quoted on the record jacket of *On Wenlock Edge and Ten Blake Songs*, EMI HQS 1236, 1971.

19. E 717; K 172. I have attempted to show what the drafts reveal about the poem in 'Blake's revision of the Tyger', *Publications of the Modern Language Association of America*, lxxi (1956), 669–85.

20. Raine, II, 31.

21. Bentley, *Blake Records*, p. 286.

22. George Whalley, *Poetic Process* (Cleveland and New York, 1697).

Chapter 4. 'The Marriage of Heaven and Hell'

1. E 34; K 149. Page references in discussions of shorter works when obvious will be ommitted.

2. A. C. Swineburne, *William Blake: A Critical Study* (London, 1906).

3. Henry Crabb Robinson, *Diary, Reminiscences, and Correspondence*, third ed. (London, 1872), II, 9 (10 Dec. 1825).

4. Quotations from Swedenborg are from *Heaven and Its Wonders, and Hell: From Things Seen and Heard*, rev. F. Bailey (London, 1909), p. 188 (sec. 589).

5. *Letters*, pp. 38–9.

6. Pierre Bayle, *Dictionnaire historique et critique*, of which there were English editions in 1710, 1734–8, 1734–41, and 1826.

7. E 267; K 778.

8. Theodor Gomperz, *Greek Thinkers: A History of Ancient Philosophy* (New York, 1908) I, 71.

9. Frye, p. 201.

10. Erdman, *Blake: Prophet*, pp. 202, 210.

11. Colin Maclaurin, *Sir Isaac Newton's Philosophical Discoveries* (London, 1750); Richard Payne Knight, *A Discourse on the Worship of Priapus and Its Connections with the Mystical Theology of the Ancients*, new ed. (London, 1952), pp. 24–31, 91, 109, 185; Coleridge, *Letters*, II, 865–6; Shelley, *The Complete Poetical Works*, Ed. Thomas Hutchinson (Oxford, 1934), pp. 784–5.

12. E 585; K 81.

13. Gilchrist, p. 317.

14. E 540; K 585.

Chapter 5. Political prophecies

1. Erdman, *Blake: Prophet*, p. 153.

2. ibid., pp. 164–174 especially.

3. Pierre Berger, *William Blake, Poet and Mystic*, trans. Daniel Connor (New York, 1915), p. 333.

4. E 606; K 392.

5. E 607; K 392.

6. In his edition of *The Poetical Works of William Blake* (London, 1905), p. 120n.

7. E 490; K 185.

8. Erdman, *Blake: Prophet*, pp. 265–9.

9. ibid., p. 202.

10. Edmund Burke, *Reflections on the Revolution in France*, Ed. William B. Todd (New York, 1959), p. 38.

11. ibid., p. 93.

12. See the critical commentary by Harold Bloom in E 817, and his reading of this work in *Blake's Apocalypse* (Ithaca, New York, 1970).

13. Erdman, *Blake: Prophet*, pp. 224, 227.

14. Raine, I, 351, 425.

Chapter 6. The shorter prophecies

1. E 43; K 158.

2. E 555; K 617.

3. E 131; K 521.

4. Blake's concept of limits may be an ironic reaction to Newton's calculus for 'fluxions'. See my article, 'Negative sources in Blake', in *William Blake: Essays for S. Foster Damon*, Ed. Alvin H. Rosenfeld (Providence, R. I., 1969), pp. 303–18. Donald Ault examines Blake's response to Newton in great depth in *Visionary Physics* (Chicago, 1974).

5. E 27; K 217.

Chapter 7. 'The Four Zoas'

1. Frye, p. 269.

2. The huge folio facsimile of the MS edited by G. E. Bentley Jr, *Vala or the Four Zoas* (Oxford, 1963), is invaluable for serious study of the poem.

3. H. M. Margoliouth, Ed., *William Blake's Vala: Blake's Numbered Text* (Oxford, 1956).

4. *Biographia Literaria*, Ed. J. Shawcross (London, 1907), II, 6.

5. Frye, p. 273.

6. Frye, pp. 277–8.

7. Page references to *The Four Zoas* will be given parenthetically, to other works in this chapter in notes.

8. E 149; K 626.

9. E 53; K 199.

10. E 104; K 491–2.

11. Erdman, *Blake: Prophet*, pp. 319–20.

12. ibid., pp. 311–12.

13. On Burnet, see Nurmi, 'Negative sources', cited in note 4 of the preceding chapter.

14. See Florian Cajori, *A History of the Conceptions of Limits and Fluxions*

in Great Britain from Newton to Woodhouse (Chicago and London, 1919).

15. Erdman, *Blake: Prophet*, p. 194.

16. Ault, *Visionary Physics*; see also Nurmi, 'Negative Sources', cited in note 4 of preceding chapter.

17. Thomas Burnet, *The Sacred Theory of the Earth*, reprinted (Carbondale, Ill., 1965), Book I, chap. ix, p. 91.

Chapter 8. The last prophecies

1. Bentley, *Blake Records*, p. 266.

2. Florence Sandler, 'The iconoclastic enterprise: Blake's Critique of "Milton's Religion",' *Blake Studies*, V (1972), 16.

3. Hayley is very much in Blake's mind here. The biographical element in this section is brought in by Bloom in *Blake's Apocalypse*.

4. See E 728 for a discussion of the order of plates. Plates 3, 4, 5 are later additions. Frye suggests reading the narrative through plates: 2, 7, 4, 6, 3, 8. An important discussion not only of the Bard's song but *Milton* as a whole is Frye's 'Notes for a Commentary on *Milton*', in V. de Sola Pinto, Ed. *The Divine Vision* (London, 1957).

5. Damon, *Dictionary*, p. 403, has Rintrah killing Thulloh, but if so Rintrah would be guilty and deserve the judgment. The pronoun antecedent for 'he smote' is Satan.

6. Frye, p. 259.

Suggestions for further reading

Bibliography

The amount of published material on Blake has become enormous. Attempts to furnish guides through it are found in the introductory essay, 'Blake's reputation and interpreters', in G. E. Bentley Jr and Martin K. Nurmi, *A Blake Bibliography* (Minneapolis, 1964), which is the only modern bibliography with pretensions to any degree of completeness (though it omits reviews and shorter notices); and in the bibliographical essay, 'Blake', in C. W. and L. H. Houtchens, Eds., *The English Romantic Poets and Essayists*, rev. ed. (New York, 1966), the essay originally written by Northrop Frye and brought up to date by Martin K. Nurmi. Current bibliography of Blake appears annually, with critiques, in 'The Romantic movement: A selective and critical bibliography', in *English Language Notes*. Bibliographical information also appears in *The Blake Newsletter*. Still of great value is Sir Geoffrey Keynes, *A Bibliography of William Blake* (New York, 1921). Since each of Blake's illuminated books is unique, a census of copies is valuable, and that by Sir Geoffrey Keynes and Edwin Wolf II, *William Blake's Illuminated Books: A Census* (New York, 1953), while needing to be brought up to date, is useful.

Texts

There are two standard texts, both good but different. One is *The Poetry and Prose of William Blake*, Ed. David V. Erdman with critical commentary by Harold Bloom (Garden City, New York, 1965—the third printing includes minor revisions), and this gives Blake's text without editorial modifications, preserving his idiosyncratic punctuation—or lack of it. It includes some letters. The other is *The Complete Writings of William Blake, with variant readings*, Ed. Geoffrey Keynes (London, 1966), an edited text with punctuation added and including the letters. Primary texts for works in illuminated printing—though there are textual variants from one copy to another, noted especially in Erdman's edition—are the hand-stencil coloured facsimiles issued by the Trianon Press for the Blake Trust during the past two decades. Facsimiles of two works left in MS, *Tiriel* and *Vala or the Four Zoas*, have been edited and published by G. E. Bentley Jr, both by the Clarendon Press. A revised edition of *The Letters of William Blake*, Ed. Geoffrey Keynes, including letters to Blake, appeared in 1970. An annotated edition of *The Poems of William Blake* (London, 1971), Ed. W. H. Stevenson, based on the Erdman text but modifying it, gives useful annotations at the foot of the page, but it does not include the prose. Peculiar to Blake are those series of illustrations to the words of others which comment as much as they illustrate, the illustrations to Job and Dante, for instance, being exegesis and literary criticism, respectively. But these are beyond our scope.

Biographies

Still the best biography is Alexander Gilchrist, *Life of William Blake*, Ed. with notes by Ruthven Todd (London, 1942 [and after]). Mona Wilson, *The Life of William Blake* (London, 1971), was first published in 1927, revised in 1948 and again in 1971 and therefore includes the most recent information. An invaluable compendium of biographical documents is G. E. Bentley Jr, *Blake Records* (Oxford: 1969).

Criticism

Blake has been very fortunate in his critics, and rather than try to select from all the criticism I shall mention a few influential general books. S. Foster Damon, *William Blake, His Philosophy and Symbols* (Boston, 1924 [subsequently reprinted]), a pioneering book still of value; Northrop Frye, *Fearful Symmetry* (Princeton, 1947 [reissued, Boston, 1965, with a new preface but not revised]), of great importance; David V. Erdman, *Blake: Prophet against Empire* (Princeton, 1954), revised edition, Garden City, New York, 1969, a very full and enormously detailed study of Blake in his own time and especially of his historical allegory; Harold Bloom, *Blake's Apocalypse: A Study in Poetic Argument* (Garden City, New York, 1963; Ithaca, New York, 1970), an illuminating reading of the works as poetic argument. Two useful studies of Blake's thought are Peter F. Fisher, *The Valley of Vision* (Toronto, 1961) and Morton D. Paley, *Energy and Imagination* (Oxford, 1970). More specialized studies may be found through the bibliographic guides mentioned above.

There are numerous useful collections of essays on Blake, such as: V. De Sola Pinto, Ed., *The Divine Vision* (London, 1957); John E. Grant, Ed., *Discussions of William Blake* (Boston, 1961); Northrop Frye, Ed., *Blake* (Englewood Cliffs, New Jersey, 1966; Alvin H. Rosenfeld, Ed., *William Blake* (Providence, Rhode Island, 1969); David V. Erdman and John E. Grant, Eds., *Blake's Visionary Forms Dramatic* (Princeton, 1970); Stuart Curran and Anthony Wittreich, Eds., *Blake's Sublime Allegory* (Madison, Wis., 1973); Morton D. Paley and Michael Phillips, Eds., *William Blake* (Oxford, 1973).

Other reference works

A two-volume *Concordance to the Writings of William Blake*, ed. David V. Erdman (Ithaca, New York, 1967) gives references to the Keynes text but incorporates textual revisions made with the help of a team of Blake scholars. The revisions are incorporated in the Erdman text and most of them also in the latest Keynes text. S. Foster Damon's *A Blake Dictionary* (Providence, Rhode Island, 1965) contains useful notes and short articles on a wide variety of topics. It is no mere reference work but an interpretive encyclopaedia by a strong-minded critic and should be used as such.

Periodicals and societies

Two periodicals are devoted exclusively to Blake: *Blake Studies*, begun 1967 and published semi-annually from Illinois State University, Normal, Ill. 61761; and *Blake Newsletter*, begun about the same time, published quarterly under the sponsorship of the Dept. of English, University of New Mexico, Albuquerque, N. M. 87106, which publishes news, notes, articles, and reviews. The American Blake Foundation, located at Illinois State University, is also publishing semi-annually a new series, *Materials for the Study of Blake: A Facsimile Series for the General Reader,* some of the volumes of which are projected to be in colour (available in Great Britain from Faustus Bibliographics Ltd in Hampstead, as is *Blake Studies*). The Blake Trust in England was founded to issue the facsimile editions of the illuminated books through the Trianon Press.

Index

NOTE: This is a selective index. Only principal references to works,
characters, and topics are included.

Adam, 77, 101, 137
Adams, Franklin P., 94
Africa, 89, 101–2, 144
Ahania, 25, 116–17, 120–1
Albion, 25–6, 120–2, 128
Albion's Prince, 23
All Religions Are One, 18, 51–7
America, 22, 23, 86–91, 100, 138
America: A Prophecy, 23–4, 41, 87–
  91, 102
'Ancient of Days', 33, 140
'Ancients', 31, 33
Androgyne, 121
Angels, 82–4, 91
Antiquities of Athens, 23
Apocalypse, 44, 56, 60–1, 75, 91–3,
  115, 144–5, 160
Archbishop of Paris, 87
Aristotle, 83, 108
Asia, 101–2
Astle, Thomas, 45
Ault, Donald, 165–6

Bach, J. S., 66–7
Bacon, Francis, 51–4, 57, 73, 159
Barlow, Joel, 23
Basire, James, 14, 18, 43
Bastille, 85–7
Bath, 159
Bayle, Pierre, 73
Beethoven, Ludwig van, 161
Bentley, G. E., Jr, 16, 33, 162–6
Bereton, William, 159
Berger, Pierre, 86

Berkeley, George, 137
Beulah, 125–7, 131–3
Bible, 25, 105, 156, and *passim*
'Bible of Hell', 25, 83–4, 105, 116,
  118
Bishop, Morchard (Oliver Stoner),
  162
Blair, Robert, 30
Blake, Catherine, 16–17, 21, 28, 33,
  48, 141
Blake, James (brother), 30
Blake, Robert (brother), 16, 18, 45,
  47, 50
Blake, William: family, 13–14;
  education and apprenticeship, 14–
  15; as artist and engraver, 23, 27,
  30, 31, 32, 33, 43, 82; as radical,
  22; residences, 25, 27–9, 32, 105,
  154; trial for sedition, 22, 27–9,
  155; visionary faculty, 14, 15–16,
  31; death, 33
Bloom, Harold, 100, 156, 166
Boehme, Jacob, 21, 66, 76
Book of Ahania, The, 25, 116–17
Book of Los, The, 25, 117–18
Book of Thel, The, 18, 68–9
Bowen, Thomas, 159
Bromion, 103–4
Bronowski, Jacob, 163
Brown, Palmer, 163
Bunhill Fields, 14, 33
Bunyan, John, 31, 33
Bürger, Gottfried Augustus, 27
Burgundy, Duke of, 87

Burke, Edmund, 97–8
Burnet, Thomas, 136, 140
Butts, Thomas, 27, 32
Byron, George Gordon, Lord, 12, 32

Cajori, Florian, 165
Calvin, John, 21
Canada, 89
Carroll, Lewis (Charles Dodgson), 46
Chatterton, Thomas, 41, 43, 46, 78
Chaucer, Geoffrey, 30, 31
'Chimney Sweeper, The', 61–2
Chimney Sweeping, 61
Chopin, Frédéric, 89
Christ, 24, 77, 83, 95, 98–9, and *passim*; *see also* Jesus
Church of England, 33
Cock, John, 28–9, 159
Coleridge, S. T., 22, 39, 58, 79, 120
Collins, William, 47
Compass points, 158–9
'Contemplation', 43
Contraries, 21, 65, 70–84, 111–16, 125, 148–56, 160
'Couch of Death', 43
Council of God, 123
Cowper, William, 27
Cromek, Robert, 30
Crucifixion, 141–2, 161
'Crystal Cabinet, The', 99, 125
Cumberland, George, 16, 27, 31
Cumberland, George [Jr], 28, 31
Cunningham, Alan, 31
Cycles, 93, 131, 150, 156–9

Damon, S. Foster, 165
Dante (Dante Alighieri), 15, 33
Darwin, Erasmus, 23
Daughters of Albion, 159
Defoe, Daniel, 46
Deism, 144
Descartes, 80, 139
Descriptive Catalogue, 20, 30
Diogenes, 80
Drama, 15, 32, 42–3

Eden, 124–7, 131, 152–3
Edward III, 42; see also *King Edward the Third*
Egremont, Countess of, 30
'Elect', 150
Elijah, 83
Ellis, John, 14
Emanations, 121–2, 154–6
England, Martha, 46
Enion, 120–1, 131
Enitharmon, 25, 95, 98–101, 112–113, 120–1, 148, 152
Erdman, David V., 13, 22, 41, 43, 76, 88, 97, 99–101, 103, 123, 134–135, 140
Eternals, 107–10, 123
Eternity, *see* Eden
Europe, 33 (frontispiece), 23, 95–101, 102
Exhibition of 1809, 30–1
Ezekiel, 80, 160

'Fair Elenor', 40–1
Fairchild, Hoxie Neale, 164
Fayette (LaFayette), 87
Female Will, 93, 100, 121, 129–30
First Book of Urizen, The, 25–6
Fisher, Peter F., 126–7
Flaxman, John, 16, 45, 72, 85
Foote, Samuel, 56
Forster, E. M., 11, 63
Four Zoas, The, 20, 29, 90, 118, 119–145
Fourfold Vision, 124–7
France, 22, 76, 82, 101, 134
Franklin, Benjamin, 90
Freher, Andreas, 21
French, Blake's study of, 15
French Revolution, The, 20, 22, 28, 85–7
Frye, Northrop, 19, 76, 119, 120–1, 124–5, 160, 163
Furnaces, 156–9
Fuseli, Henry, 16, 23, 147
Fuzon, 116–17

Gates, Horatio, 90

Gates of Paradise, The (For Children . . . and For the Sexes), 23
Generation, 126–7
George III, 88–92, 101, 138
Ghost of Abel, The, 32
Ghost of a Flea' The', 31
Gilbert, W. S., 46
Gilchrist, Alexander, 18, 164
Ginsberg, Allen, 13
Gnosticism, 66
Godwin, William, 22
Golgonooza, 132, 144, 147, 154
Gomperz, Theodor, 164
Good and evil, 70–1
Gordon Riots, 16
Gordred, 41–2
Grant, John E., 13, 163
Greek, Blake's study of, 27
Greene, Nathaniel, 90
Griggs, E. L., 162
Guillotine, 42
'Gwin, King of Norway', 40–2

Hagstrum, Jean, 13
Haley, William, 27–30, 72, 146, 149, 155, 159, 162, 166
Hancock, John, 90
Handel, G. F., 47–48
Hardy, Thomas, 104
Hawkins, John, 18
Haymarket Theatre, 46
Hayter, S. W., 50
Hebrew, Blake's study of, 27
Hegel, G. W. F., 75
Henry V, 42
Heraclitus, 75
Hermeticism, 66
Hesketh, Lady, 27
'Holy Thursday', 58
Homer, 31
Hunt, Leigh and Robert, 159
Hunter, John, 46–7
Hutchinson, Thomas, 164
Hutton (probably George Hulton), 159

Illuminated printing, 18–20, 25, 32, 50, 80, 106–7, 161

Imagination, 54–6
'Infant Joy', 58, 62
'Infant Sorrow', 58–9
Innocence and Experience, 57–62
Ionesco, Eugene, 46
Isaiah, 77, 80, 127
Island in the Moon, The, 17–18, 45–9
Israel, 160
Italian, Blake's study of, 15, 33

Jenkins, Herbert, 33
Jerusalem, 25, 26, 121, 144, 148, 160
Jerusalem, 28, 29, 147, 156–61
Jesus, 44, 56, 58, 107–8, 117, 123, 124, 133–4, 141, 153, 158, 160
Job engravings, 32
John, 127
Johnson, Joseph, 22, 85
Johnson, Samuel, 46–7
Jonah, 88

Katterfelto, Gustavus, 45–6
Keynes, Geoffrey, 13, 99, 162, 163
King Edward the Third, 43, 46
Knight, Richard Payne, 79

Lamb, Charles, 31, 66
'Lamb, The', 62–3, 66
Lambeth Books, 25
Last Judgement, The, 30, 144
Last Supper, The, 27
Lavater, John Casper, 52
Law, William, 73
Lawrence, Thomas, 32
Leviathan, 82
Limits, 110, 137
Linnell, John, 31–3
'Little Black Boy, The', 59–61, 102
'Little Girl Found, The', 62
'Little Girl Lost, The', 62
Locke, John, 51–2, 57, 101, 106
Los, 25, 29, 110–12, 116–18, 120–1, 128, 147, 156–8
Louis XVI, 42
Lowery, Margaret Ruth, 44, 163
Lucretius, 118
Luvah, 120–2, 123, 130, 148, 156–60

Maclaurin, Colin, 79
'Mad Song', 36–8
Man, *see* Albion
Margoliouth, H. M., 26, 119
Marriage of Heaven and Hell, The, 20–2, 70–84
Marx, Groucho (Julius), 46
Mathew, A. S., 17
Mathew, Harriet, 17, 45
'Memory hither come', 38–9
'Mental Traveller, The', 58
Mexico, 89
Michael, 152
Milton, John, 23–4, 29, 43, 78, 98–9, 136, 141, 146–56
Milton, 26, 27, 146–56
Mohammud, 101
Moore, Donald K., 162
Moses, 116
Music, 15, 19–20, 33, 36–9, 47–8, 63, 66, 89, 99, 134, 138
Mystery, 141, 144
Myth, 19, 22, 23, 25, 29–30, 91–5, 105–16, 125

Napoleon, 28, 134
Nature, 43–4, 49, 80, 90, 126–7, 130, 139
Necker, Jacques, 87
Negations, 65, 70, 75, 115–16, 149–156, 160; *see also* Contraries
Negro, 102; *see also* Africa
New Church, *see* Swedenborg
Newton, Isaac, 51–2, 57, 79, 81, 101, 137, 158, 165
Nineveh, 88
Nobodaddy, 74, 93–4, 124
Norway, 41
Notebook, The, 18, 23–4, 64
Numerology, 124–6
Nurmi, Ruth, 37–8

Ololon, 154–6
'One Man', *see* Jesus
Oothoon, 103–4
Opie, Amelia, 60
Orc, 23, 25, 40, 89–91, 102, 107, 112–13, 120–1, 148

Orléans, Duke of, 87
Ossian (James Macpherson), 43, 103

Paine, Thomas, 22, 85, 90
Palamabron, 149–54
Palmer, Samuel, 34, 72
Paracelsus (Theophrastus von Hohenheim), 72–3
Parker, James, 18, 45
Pars, Henry, 14
Paul, 127
Peachey, John, 159
Perception, 54–6, 76–84
Peru, 89
Phillips, Ambrose, 32
Pitt, William (the younger), 97, 101
Pity, 111–12
Plato, 106
Poetical Sketches, 15, 17, 19, 20, 35–45
Politics, 22–3, 24, 28, 41, 85
Pope, Alexander, 15, 73–4
Predestination, 21
Priestley, Joseph, 45
Prophecy, 88
'Proverbs of Hell', 79
Pythagoreans, 73

Rahab, 143–4
Raine, Kathleen, 13, 66, 102
'Redeemed', 150
Religion, 54–6, and *passim*
'Reprobate', 150
Reuben, 160
Revelation, 127
Reynolds, Joshua, 15–16
Richard the Lion-Hearted, 31
Richmond, Duke of, 29
Rintrah, 76, 149–54
Robinson, H. C., 31, 66
Romney, George, 18
Rose, Samuel, 29
Rosenfeld, Alvin, 165
Rousseau, Jean-Jacques, 101
Royal Academy, 15, 18, 27

Sampson, John, 93
'Samson', 43–4

Sandler, Florence, 148
Satan, 78, 94, 136–7, 149–54, and *passim*
Satire, 17–18, 20, 42–3, 45–9, 70–84
Scholfield, John, 28–9, 159
'Schoolboy, The', 62
Schubert, Franz, 57
Scotland, 159
Seven Eyes of God, 135
Sex, 39–40, 68, 91, 95–7, 102–4
'Sexual', 89–90, 98–9, 112, 121, 125–126, 129–31
Shadowy Daughter of Urthona, 89–90, 92, 95–6
Shadowy Female, 95–8, 143–4
Shawcross, John, 165
Shelley, P. B., 12, 79
'Sick Rose, The', 67–8
Sieyès, Abbé de, 87
Simpson, Louis, 12
Slavery, 59–61, 103–4
Smith, J. T., 15, 36
Snyder, Gary, 13
'Song of Liberty, A', 84
Song of Los, The, 25, 101–2
Songs of Innocence, 18, 20, 48
Songs of Innocence and of Experience, 19, 24–5, 57–68
Sons of Albion, 159
Sophia, Princess, 33
Spectre, 132–3, 137, **141**
Spectre of Tharmas, 131
Spectre of Urthona, 148
Spenser, Edmund, 35, 73, **103**
Stars, 40, 66, 87
Starry heavens, 97–8
States, 107, 143
Stedman, John Gabriel, 23, 102–3
Stothard, Thomas, 16, 30
Sullivan, Arthur, 46
Swedenborg, Emanuel, 20, 70–84, 164
Swift, Jonathan, 93
Swinburne, A. C., 70
Symons, Arthur, 162
'System', 51–6, 70–1

Tatham, Frederick, 33
Ten Commandments, 83, 91
Tharmas, 120–1, 128, 131–2, 148, 158–9
Theotormon, 103–4
There Is No Natural Religion, 18, 51–7
Thomson, James, 40
Thornton, Robert John, 32
Thullo, 152
'Tiriel', 19, 93
'To Autumn', 39–40
'To Morning', 40
'To Spring', 39–40, 66–7
'To Summer', 39–40
'To the Evening Star', 40
'To Winter', 39–40
Todd, Ruthven, 50, 162
Trusler, Rev. John, 27, 126
Tulk, C. A., 58
'Tyger, The', 12, 62–6, 91

Ulro, 127
Urizen, 23, 25, 40, 74, 93–4, 103, 105–18, 120–2, 124, 129–30, 148, 152, 158
Urthona, 91, 94–5, 120–1, 158

Vala, 119–22, 148, 160
Vala, 25–7; see also *The Four Zoas*
Varley, John, 31
Vaughan, Thomas, 158
Vaughan Williams, Ralph, 63
Vaughan Williams, Ursula, 164
Virgil, 32
Visionary heads, 31, 43
Visions of the Daughters of Albion, 23, 102–4
'Voice of the Bard, The', 62
Voltaire (François Arouet), 46, 101
Vortexes, 139–40, 142

Wainwright, Thomas, **147**
Wales, 140
Wales, Prince of, 46
'War Song to Englishmen, A', 35, 43

Ward, James, 32
Warner, Rev. Richard, 159
Warren, Joseph, 90
Washington, George, 90, 91
Wedgwood pottery, 31
Whalley, George, 67, 164
Wheels, *see* Cycles
Wicksteed, Joseph, 13

Woodcuts, 32
Wordsworth, William, 22, 57, 120

Yeats, W. B., 14, 74
Young, Edward, 26–7, 122

Zoas, 30, 120–1, 148, 160, 161; see
    also *The Four Zoas*

ERRATA

It was not possible in this publication of the present book to make corrections in the text, but I wish to correct here one very major error and several lesser ones. It was erroneously but very confidently reported to me that Sir Geoffrey Keynes had passed away, so in haste and without proper checking the word "late" was prefixed to his name, on pp. 13 and 99, out of respect for that great scholar. I am happy indeed to be able to correct that unfortunate error, for which Sir Geoffrey kindly forgave me. In addition, the following errors should be corrected:

p. 18, line 7: for "in those a rare bird" read "in those days a rare bird."

p. 19, line 10: for "Contrasting" read "Contrary."

p. 21, line 30: for "corruscating" read "coruscating."

p. 23, line 11: for "1794" read "1793."

p. 24, line 25: delete "back and forth."

p. 57, line 16: for "regards" read "regard."

p. 59, line 29: for "abolished in 1810" read "declared illegal in 1807 and made a felony in 1811."

p. 74, line 5: for "Nobo-daddy" read "Nobodaddy."

p. 83, line 37: for "angel and devil embrace" read "angel embraces the fire and emerges as Elijah."

p. 87, line 32: for "1790" read "1790 or 1791."

p. 91, lines 10–13: for "The Prince of Albion . . . Washington's feet" read: "Albion's Angel calls for war trumpets, but the thirteen rebelious angels are no longer loyal; they are 'indignant burning with the fires of Orc,' and, rending their robes of allegiance, they descend to stand with Washington, Paine, and Warren. The thirteen colonial governors, helpless in 'mental chains,' grovel at Washington's feet." The reading in the text is badly mixed up.

p. 146, line 13: for "treason" read "sedition."

p. 164, n. 2 (chap. 4): for "Swineburne" read "Swinburne."